I Hope You're Listening, God

I Hope You're Listening, God

A Prayer Journal

ANDREW M. GREELEY

A Crossroad Book
The Crossroad Publishing Company
New York

1997

The Crossroad Publishing Company
370 Lexington Avenue, New York, NY 10017

Printed in the United States of America

Library of Congress Catalog Card Number: 97-69107
ISBN 0-8245-1691-5

May 1995

May 5, 1995 — Chicago

My Love,

The ordination class reunion was gratifying. We are now old enough, I think, to put any rivalry behind us. No one seems to mind anymore that I turned out to be a "celebrity," and I am grateful for that. It didn't help though when some of the lay people present wanted autographs.

We get older, much older indeed, but life goes on, and I thank You for the grace of my life and again for the fact that it has been so exciting, more than I could have ever dreamed.

What a forty-one years! I couldn't help thinking about my obituary this morning as I went through the paper. I assume that it is already written and is filled with the usual clichés. But so what? I have worked hard and had an enormous impact, and that's what being a priest is about. No doubt the impact wasn't of the sort I expected forty-one years ago in the bitter cold at Mundelein, but the things I've become were not things I sought. They just happened. You planned them, I didn't. I'm not complaining, my Love. I think You blessed me twice, once with a vocation and again with the vocation to be the kind of priest I am. I did not choose. *You* chose. Sometimes I have not responded well, and for that I'm sorry. I've made a lot of messes because of weariness and anger and discouragement and frustration. For those I'm sorry too. But I've helped a lot of people through Your grace, and for that I'm glad and grateful.

There are not many anniversaries left, but that's all right too. Mortality adds poignancy to our human condition. Mortality gives it direction and purpose, as bitter as it may sometimes seem. As I pray through this computer, I believe that You are the one I encounter in these interludes of loving joy each day. And I believe that such love and joy can never end.

So I love You and will always love You and will celebrate today more joyously than ever Your great gift of priesthood to me. My theology of what it is to be a priest may have changed somewhat, but my new view enhances priesthood rather than diminishing it, so I am more grateful than ever.

I love You. Help me to love You more. And please, help all priests.

May 8, 1995 — Chicago

My Love,

VE day. I don't remember where I was on that day some fifty years ago. I do remember being happy to know the war was over. Forty million people died, each one of them, as President Clinton said today, a personal tragedy. How You must have suffered with them! And war continues throughout the world though Western Europe for the first time in a couple of thousand years is at peace and

for the first time in half a millennium there are no armies
marching through it.

Thank You for that. And thank You for the relative
peace of the past fifty years. And for the prosperity that
has come with it.

I saw my doctor today, and he says I'm fine, still a good
fifteen years younger than my age. Help me to take care
of the gift of health You have given me and to make good
use of however many days I have in the future.

And I'm sorry for the hypochondria of the past week
or two, though there were some reasons for it. Anyway it's
nice to know that I'm still in good shape.

I love You.

May 9, 1995 — Chicago

My Love,

I've been reading the *Scarecrow Poetry* book — songs
from post-middle age. What sad and dreary stuff—utterly
without hope! How can people live that way. I guess the
answer is that they don't live all that well, poor souls. I
am so thankful that You've given me hope — as well as
energy and good health. I suppose that when the last two
go hope may weaken. But as long as You sustain me, my
hope will never go.

What can be done about those who have no hope?

I think I'd like to write something for them, but how
would that be done?

None of the poets I've read so far seems to see any
wisdom acquired in age — no new graces, no new love,
nothing. But above all none, not a single one so far has any
faith in the future, nor any sense of transcendence over
death. One of the poets, watching a husband and wife do

a piano duet, laments that they were children once. As were we all. And now they are sixty.

Truly, but is that all that is to be said? One hopes not or life is a bitter tease.

I don't believe it is. I feel like screaming at them that they are all wrong.

But am I right? I think that I am, but if so, that too is grace.

I love You. Help me, help all of us, to see Your grace.

May 11, 1995 — Chicago

My Love,

A slight beam of hope in the poems for today. A mother sees signs of joy in her daughter's tenderness in helping her with make-up. Not much but something.

I love You. If only I wasn't so sleepy.

May 13, 1995 — Chicago

My Love,

Despite the clouds and the rain spring is sneaking into Chicago. Trees are blooming and everything is lovely. I love You, on this Mother's Day eve, You who are my mother as well as my Father and always my Love.

May 16, 1995 — Chicago

My Love,

I've spent most of the morning bumbling and stumbling and catching up on details. Ugh.

I have been able, however, to extend some of my awareness of Your presence and love beyond my periods of contemplation. They are wondrous interludes, but they do not change my life. Perhaps I shouldn't expect them to change my life right away. Or in some instances at all. I still will be tired in the morning and the evening. I'll still be limited by all the constraints of human nature in general and my own human nature in particular.

Still life should be different, and I should evidently and eventually be a different person.

I love You.

May 17, 1995 — Chicago

My Love,

I feel better this morning for reasons I can't understand. Maybe I'm free from the cold germ at last. What terrible slaves we are to our bodily weaknesses! Yet You love us as we are. You dote on us. And in that is our grounds for hope.

You do lurk everywhere, don't You? How can I let myself get deep into those moods of discouragement?

I must not let myself leave for Europe tomorrow night depressed, nor grow depressed on the trip.

Life goes on and so does Your love.

Which I, however ineptly, try to return.

I love You.

May 24, 1995 — Köln

My Love,

I'm back in one of my favorite cities — please note the appropriate umlaut above the o — and one of my favorite hotels, if only because I could go swimming today, which was wonderful and for which many thanks.

Thank You too for the time of contemplation at the airport. That establishes that I can reach You even in the worst circumstances.

The people here are so friendly. I had supper with Wolfgang and Michael, who have been good friends and are now even close friends. I thank You for this dimension of life, one more surprise from Your generosity.

I think Wolfgang and I are on to something very important in the sociology of religion. We may be able to make a major contribution, which is also a matter for much gratitude.

Thank You for all the graces of this trip. I love You.

Still, I'd rather be in Grand Beach.

May 27, 1995 — Köln

My Love,

Lightning strikes occasionally, says the poet. Yet I can encounter You every day, sometimes with special joy as today, almost at will and despite my distractions. How come? Is it You?

It has to be You, the source of all joy and peace and happiness and hope.

I love You.

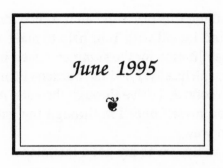

June 1995

June 4, 1995 — Grand Beach, Michigan

My Love,

I'm sorry that I have written not a word of reflection since I've come home, and not much while I was away either. I'm slowly returning to normal, but I'm still beat out. It was a hard if successful trip. A lot of work and not much time to rest. My attempts to do a daily contemplation ran out of steam. It's a pretty weak spiritual life which collapses under the relatively easy pressures of two weeks in Europe. I'm sorry. I know Your love for me is not harmed by my failures, but I am discouraged because I am so easily wiped out. I hope to retool up here, though I must go back into Chicago for Monday and Tuesday, two events I got myself into. I desperately need to slow down for a while. I love You. Help me to love You more and get back on the track.

June 5, 1995 — Grand Beach

My Love,

I made it to the beach yesterday, which was wonderful. A perfect way to begin the summer. I want to thank You today for making this place and all it stands for part of my life. I hope and intend with Your help to make it a place of rest and rehabilitation for the summer. I need it physically, emotionally, spiritually. I feel the burdens lifting from my shoulders as soon as I drive through the gate. Alas, I reimpose them on myself once I'm through the gate. Not this summer. No way.

Help me to live up to my good intentions.

I love You.

June 8, 1995 — Grand Beach

My Love,

Last night I watched the two-hour special on Irish emigrants on PBS. It was certainly done from the Irish and Catholic viewpoint, which is rare enough in TV these days. I was deeply moved by the stories and letters and pictures and songs, especially by the pictures which all seemed to be of people I know. Bright brave young people who left everything behind to run the risks of seeking a new life. Some found only sorrow and pain and early death, others did pretty well, and still others found happiness. Most of our dreams don't come true, but some do, and they are often better in the enjoyment of them than what we might have found if our early dreams had come true.

We also should realize that we stand on the shoulders of giants. We have the chances we have — I have the chances I have — because so many people who went before braved and suffered so much. I am grateful to them and to You and for what they did. May I never forget them and never forget how much I owe them.

Help me to make good use of what they made possible for me.

And please take care of Laura and Frank and Marvi.

I love You.

June 10, 1995 — Chicago

My Love,

Cardinal Bernardin has pancreatic cancer. Survival rate 10 percent. Worst-case scenario, six months to a year. Best case is that they've caught it early, which doesn't usually happen, and they can take it out.

I am devastated. He is a friend. He is the last great churchman in America. He would have shaped the next papal conclave. The next man they send here could be an Opus Dei selection and that would be a disaster for the Church. I'm not sure that I'm safe, though as You well know, even if they try to throw me out I won't go.

Joe [Cardinal Bernardin] was on TV yesterday, a priest to the end.

Everything is in Your hands as always, and You know what You're doing.

Marvin, Laura, Pastora's mother, Frank Gill, and now the Cardinal — so many people to pray for.

The day is grim and terrible, which adds to my mood of discouragement and depression.

I pray with all my heart and soul for Joe. Grant that he recovers. We need him so much.

But I accept whatever might be Your will.

I love You.

June 11, 1995 — Grand Beach

My Love,

Joe called yesterday in response to my brief fax, which was good of him to do. In effect he was saying goodbye. I said to him that we would meet again. Which of course we will. I must reconcile myself to the truth that he will be dead in a few weeks or a few months, a new bishop will come to Chicago, and who knows what will happen next?

I am so very, very sad on this grim and gray and gloomy Sunday morning.

When I came home from dinner at Erika's last night about ten I made phone calls to two friends who have terrible health problems in their families. I listened for almost an hour to anguish and offered what little support I could. One of them wondered why You demanded so much of her. "You are," she said, "not fair."

But "fairness" as we see it is not part of the game, is it?

Grant Joe — and the others — life and long life.

I love You.

June 12, 1995 — Grand Beach

My Love,

Joe's surgery is today. I beg You spare him for us. We need him, the Church needs him. Your ways are inscrutable and I intend neither to challenge them nor to try to understand them. You have been so good to me all my life that I hesitate to insist on anything.

But I wish to come as close to insistence as I can and still not offend against respect or love. If it be Your will that he be taken from us, than Your will be done. But I hope and pray and plead that it not be Your will, not yet. There is so much yet for him to do.

Please, please, please.

June 13, 1995 — Grand Beach

My Love,

I was up at 6:30, and it's been a busy morning already. Channel 5 came out to interview me about the Cardinal.

The news about him is better than it might have been. The tumor seems to have been contained. So the five-year survival rate goes up to 25 percent and the median life expectancy to three years. That's not good, but it's better than 3 percent and three months. The tumor may not be malignant. We won't know until tomorrow or the next day. However, judging by the body language at the press conference, the doctors seem to think that it isn't but are not saying anything until the final pathology report is in.

So You have given him back to us, it would seem, at least for a little time and maybe for a long time. For that I'm grateful, and I continue to beg that the tumor not be malignant and that he is restored to us for his full term of eight more years. But as I said yesterday, all is in Your hands and I trust You and love You.

June 14, 1995 — Grand Beach

My Love,

We will probably get the news about the Cardinal's pathology reports today. Please grant that all has gone well.

Ken Velo [Cardinal Bernardin's chancellor] just called. They'll know at three this afternoon and probably have a press conference at five o'clock. He'll call me before that. Again I beg You that the Cardinal will be all right.

Ken sounded discouraged, as well he might be after all the strains. He says that the Cardinal is positive but a realist. He also said that the Cardinal always expects the worst when going into a meeting. So he expects the worst. I guess that's consistent with being a realist.

These have been terrible days for me. How much more terrible for the Cardinal himself and his family and those priests like Ken who are close to him. I pray for them too.

Again I beg You that all will have gone well.

But I accept Your will.

I love You.

June 15, 1995 — Chicago

My Love,

The final news on Joe is mixed. Bottom line: five-year survival rate of 25 percent. I continue to be convinced that he will recover and will vote in the next conclave. I am grateful to You that the chances are as good as they seem to be, given his condition to begin with.

As I have argued with You all week, Chicago and the Church need him.

And he is my friend and I need him.

No matter what happens, I love You.

June 18, 1995 — Grand Beach

My Love,

It's a glorious day here. Waterskiing at Pine Lake required an hour's nap. I feel great. I hate to leave here just when summer is starting. But I must go to Ireland, where

I should have a good time too. Take care of me on the trip. I beg You. I read Bill Leonard's memoir this afternoon, very impressive. I wrote him and congratulated him on the book and on the enormous victory the liturgists won, for which much praise to You.

I am increasingly grateful to You for the peace and joy I am finding in contemplative prayer. I sit in a comfortable position, clear my mind as best I can, and then either sink into something which is the center of my being or find myself captured by it as soon as my mind is half clear. When I'm "there" I am rapidly filled with peace and joy and love. My face breaks out into a smile, my hands close over my chest, and my joy becomes so powerful that I cry out or groan or do something like that. I wince, tears form in my eyes. Yet it is not quite unbearable joy, it is not like what William James or the others describe, not quite yet anyway. I could remain there indefinitely, but my work orientation prevents that. Still I'm sad to leave. And when I open my eyes, anything that's white seems to glow at me, like the VCR cabinet or Cris Larkin's bridal dress on the TV.

I don't know what to make of this. It is not classical contemplation, but it is not, I am convinced, merely wish fulfillment. It should not be so easy to find this "center point," but that's a function of my permeable boundaries I suppose. What it is really doesn't matter. It is good and wonderful and my challenge is to recall it at least intermittently in the course of the day. Because I am convinced that it is You I meet.

Do You really love me that way? Of course You do. Help me to love You in return.

June 22, 1995 — Dublin

My Love,

How many times have I told You that You were on Your best run when You created these people? There are of course things wrong with Irish culture and with many Irish people too.

But the joy and the love of play are still unique, and one finds in it (this one anyhow) the kind of joy which should permeate all our lives.

I love You. Thanks for the graces of this trip. Help me to revel in them and this country.

June 23, 1995 — Dublin

My Love,

My talk went well yesterday. Two of my students from Chicago showed up, which was a surprise. Because of my odd life I have had very few people I can call students. It's nice to have them, however.

Supper last night at Joe Dunn's was fascinating because the senior civil servant from the Foreign Office was there. He was less optimistic on the peace process than many other people I spoke with. His most important insight was that the solutions will have to be figured out by Dublin and floated as a joint British-Irish effort. The Brits don't have the understanding of how the IRA thinks and feels to be able to cope with them. John Major's possible defeat in Parliament won't help the process.

Jet lag is pretty much over. But I still am depressed. What am I doing here, I ask myself. And what have I accomplished with my life?

I have a powerful inclination to quit, though obviously

I won't do that. Yet the word "failure" rings over and over in my head and with it the feeling that the best thing I could do would be to acknowledge that and stop trying.

There are so many reasons why it would be nice to get out of the various messes in which I have involved myself or in which people I have trusted have thrust me.

I should not be thinking this way. Or maybe I should.

Anyway I love You.

June 28, 1995 — Dublin

My Love,

What a failure this trip has been spiritually. I have kept this journal of reflections, but there's not much in it but junk. I have done no contemplation. I'm on the way home distressed and discouraged. I'm sorry. I tried, probably not hard enough. I still know that You love me, and I try to love You.

June 29, 1995 — Grand Beach

My Love,

Bad first day back. Worse than usual. All kinds of trouble. I love You. Help me to get back on track.

July 1995

July 1, 1995 — Grand Beach

My Love,

A lovely day and a good night's sleep and I feel a lot better, though I have a way to go yet. I'm still baffled by how to proceed on the novel. Help me to make the right decision and to celebrate this weekend with gratitude for the way You have blessed this country. I love You.

July 3, 1995 — Grand Beach

My Love,

Better now. All better. The weekend has been great if busy. Thank You for it, for the freedom, for the friends, for the lake and the sky and beach and all the fun and joy.

I love You.

July 4, 1995 — Grand Beach

My Love,

A few minutes of peace before another rush begins. How clever of me to schedule a week of guests right after

21

a return from Europe! How dumb can one get? Or how much a false image of omnipotence can one fabricate?

A lot about sickness the last couple of days, though I have been running so fast to keep up with the obligations of being a host that I haven't had time to think about it. My classmate Tony Novak died after long lung cancer. Be good to him. I was in Europe when it happened and couldn't make the funeral. I haven't seen him much since ordination, yet I mourn for him and for all of us. Three deaths in the last year and Frank Gill sick. Our mortality is showing up, much ahead of time.

And another friend on the phone recovering from a stroke. More energy than the last time, but still a way to go.

And then the Cardinal on the phone, sounding upbeat and vigorous. He said he'd be up here later in the summer. He'd walked twelve blocks the day he called. Many people stop him on the street to congratulate him on his apparent recovery. Spare him to us, I beg You.

I conclude from this that we are all fragile, even if I am still able to waterski and will do so shortly on Lake Michigan.

I love You. Help me to love You more as I try to ease back into a normal life.

July 5, 1995 — Grand Beach

My Love,

As I look out the window of my room here I see the flowers in my new perennial garden. They are marvelously beautiful. I regret I didn't have the garden before. I tell myself that I ought to know their names, but knowing their names wouldn't affect their beauty one way or another, would it?

If there are flowers, then You are. And the flowers are a hint of You for which I am very grateful, especially as I continue to wind down and into the summer which is supposed to be one of peace and reflection, though it hasn't become that yet, has it?

Anyway I love You. Help me to love You more.

July 6, 1995 — Grand Beach

My Love,

I have been reading Enda Lyons's book on Your Son Jesus and marvel as I read it how we have fouled up our presentation of Jesus. Many Catholics are de facto Docetists: the divinity in Jesus completely overshadows his humanity and thus the mystery of the Incarnation — and its lesson for us — is defined away. I remember the time when an investigation was ordered of our parish because some nut objected to the words "the man Jesus" in one of the Gospels. Someone from downtown came out to investigate us and, even though the reading was from the CCD translation approved by the American bishops, ended up by warning us to be careful of shocking the faithful. I don't think any of that has changed one bit. What should have worried Rome was that there could be someone who so misunderstood the nature of the Incarnation.

But the issue wasn't Your Son. The issue, as it always is, was the power of church leaders. I propose in whatever years are ahead of me to raise my voice loudly against the abuse of power in the Church.

I love You. Help me to understand Jesus better.

July 10, 1995 — Grand Beach

My Love,

I have before me the list of the fate of our ordination class. Of the thirty-one ordained for Chicago on May 5, 1954, eleven are dead, eight retired, seven are out of the "active" ministry, and four still active. Of those one is dying and another is in bad health. I am listed as in "special ministry" as are three (from other dioceses) who are bishops. A strange group in which to put me!

Anyway I love You and I welcome the opportunity to relax for a bit and to reflect on mortality and other things as well.

I love You.

July 13, 1995 — Grand Beach

My Love,

I'm having problems with the novel, and with some people, and not thinking clearly. But I'm reading poetry again, Yeats, whom I started to read last summer. The lines which caught my attention yesterday were from "The Coming of Wisdom with Time":

> *Though leaves are many, the root is one;*
> *Through all the lying days of my youth*
> *I swayed my leaves and flowers in the sun*
> *Now I may wither into the truth.*

A grim enough vision, is it not? I don't know whether I have become wise. I don't know that wisdom is the result of age. I do know that I'm getting old, that time has slipped by and that just now I am not so much wise as disillusioned and sad.

I am able to pretend that I'm not sad. I don't impose my sadness on others, but I feel it just the same, a sense that all I have done has been wasted, that I have been fighting with invisible demons that I cannot rout no matter how hard I try.

Bad news?

As Pete Rossi said a number of years ago, when was the last time there was good news?

Sorry to be so grim. Things go wrong. Everything seems to go wrong.

All I have left is Your love, and I don't always understand that very well.

But I do feel it now everyday in my moments of contemplative prayer. Without that I would be much worse.

It will all go away. Life goes on.

That perhaps is wisdom.

So too it is wisdom to say that I love You and want to love You more.

July 20, 1995 — Grand Beach

My Love,

Enda Lyons is quite good on Your being an Artist engaged in self-portraiture: "The Artist as a Young God" (doesn't say that, I do). Of course You are young, always so. I don't like pictures of You as an older person because eternity doesn't mean old but forever young.

So the flowers in my garden, the sky, the birds, people — all are attempts on Your part to disclose what You're like. Jesus is Your Word incarnate. Quite a neat idea and brilliant artistry. But alas how badly we have disfigured him and You through the centuries.

I continue to be tired and discouraged. But I love You.

July 24, 1995 — Chicago

My Love,

I'm in Chicago for a wedding and a couple of baptisms and some sick calls. One of the calls was to a woman whom I knew long ago and had a crush on in grammar school days. She's had a hard life, which for reasons You understand, I have been present at in some key times. Her health is poor, and she's not at all well. As I rode up the elevator, I lamented what she has had to endure. But when I left the hospital room, I felt much better. Age and suffering have not changed her all that much. Same smile, same laugh, same wit, same admirable woman.

Grace once more.

Life is stronger than death.

And love is too.

I love You.

July 27, 1995 — Grand Beach

My Love,

Chicago tonight for Frank Gill's funeral. Grant him eternal peace and joy. So much sadness. So much pain.

I have been reading, as You know, Heinrich Böll these last weeks. A truly great novelist. His stories about the horrors of war are quite powerful. War is so ugly. How do we get into it? Why all the terror and death in Bosnia? If You are a strange sort of God, as my theologian friends were saying the other night, so we are a strange sort of image and likeness of God.

Some people have to suffer so terribly.

And I have been, so far in my life, relatively immune from all but minor suffering. Why?

Mind You, I don't mind. I'm just baffled.

But You love all of us with an overwhelming love — which is strange of You too.

I love You.

July 28, 1995 — On the way to D.C.

My Love,

Frank Gill's funeral last night. Deeply moving.

There seemed a troubling unease about it all, as our class counts it's fourteenth dead out of thirty-one — with a few more sick unto death. It wasn't merely that a pilgrimage which began in 1942 in class 1C had lost another of its few remaining members. But that just now the pilgrimage seems so problematic. The priesthood and the Church have changed so much as to be almost unrecognizable. We started out on one pilgrimage and found ourselves, without much warning, on another. So nostalgia and a sense of loss permeated the room.

To tell the truth, my Love, I don't understand any of it, mostly because it deals with mortality, my own as well as his, and the overloading of my life with responsibilities, not all of which I can keep up with.

Anyway I love You and I believe in Your love.

August 2, 1995 — Grand Beach

My Love,

I circumnavigated the lake this morning on skis, so I guess I am still in good condition. Thanks much for the fun.

Learned lots of theology from Shags [John Shea], as I always do. Particularly about reading scripture. I'm going to try that again with his method in mind.

Reading Augustine I understand that You are the only important reality and the one I should concentrate on in this busy life. You are the ultimate goodness, and I should never forget that, even when I have so many other things to worry about.

You, the source of peace and joy and happiness and love I encounter in my reflections on the beach.

I love You. Help me to love You more.

August 4, 1995 — Grand Beach

My Love,

We're still caught in some kind of tropical humidity which means clouds and rain. Very grim. As was yesterday with a death bed visit, a funeral, and a wake. There's a lesson in all of this for me. Life ends in death, a simple enough conclusion.

Therefore...

Therefore, what?

Therefore I should not let little things deprive me of peace or interfere with my relationship with You.

Therefore I should live my life with as much enthusiasm as I can and thereby reflect Your exuberance and my faith that life is stronger than death.

We will all be young again, we will all laugh again.

That I must believe with all my heart and mind.

Even though it is difficult at times.

Anyway, I must also be grateful for all the good things You've given me and accept whatever You have in store for me.

I love You.

August 6, 1995 — Grand Beach

My Love,

My take on this lovely August Sunday is that all human realities given time go badly, wisdom from the late Gus Weigel. Another way to say the same thing is that we all die.

During the Mass for Jean yesterday, various scenes from her life flashed through my mind, the last scene being the casket in the church. She meant so much to so many people and what she gave of her life to all of them was now over.

Is not this, however, the scenario for all of us, with only some modifications in the story line? As I said in my homily at Mass yesterday, we prove who we are and what we believe not in times of glory but in times of suffering. It is precisely in the suffering that the glory shows itself. Eventually.

My last image of Jean was of her as a young woman again in glory.

There is no escape from tragedy. What might look in her life like decline and fall is really a quest for glory, and a successful one at that.

I must ponder these things in love.

August 9, 1995 — Grand Beach

My Love,

A grim, dark, heavy day. You know what this kind of weather does to me. I hope to begin my poetry this afternoon. Better late than never.

Marilyn said to me the other day when the phone was ringing and the doorbell was ringing and I was trying to juggle many different things at the same time that this was the life I chose and that there was no escaping the constant harassment unless I changed my style completely. Doubtless that is the truth, but it makes the kind of core work I do more difficult. I race each morning to clear my desk of the stuff that must be done so I can finish by noon. I hate that, but it comes with the territory, and I should be glad that I have an opportunity at noon to relax and reflect.

Which brings me to my principal reflection for the day: I wonder why it took so long for me to discover the capacity I have for (low level) contemplative prayer, prayer which floods my soul with peace and joy and love. Certainly there were hints before of that possibility, which I never seemed to recognize. I thank You that I now do recognize it and can steal away from everything to encounter You if not quite at will at least often and with some ease.

The challenge now, as I have said before, is to try to remember at least bits and pieces of those interludes during the course of the day, so that my contemplation may permeate, however imperfectly, the rest of my life. I haven't got very skilled at doing that, but I know that with Your help, I can do it. White, with which I'm surrounded here in my office, is part of the secret. Please help me.

I love You.

August 10, 1995 — Grand Beach

My Love,

There are no good ways to die. Some are worse than others. Consider the deaths I have encountered in the last week — heart bleeding after surgery, multiple myeloma, liver cancer. Consider that one out of three of us will eventually die of cancer. (I'm telling myself to consider, not You!). All pretty ugly — prolonged, painful, degrading.

Ugh!

How will I die?

That may be a more important question than when. But I know the answer to neither of these questions and must accept in faith whatever and whenever You have death in store for me.

The answer to all of this is that You take on human form so that You might show us how to die and that You walked into the valley of death with us so that we know we won't die alone.

This is all I have to sustain me, all that I will ever have to sustain me. But then what more could I ask for or expect?

Life ends ugly, no getting away from that. But the ugliness is not final, that too I must believe.

And then live as best I can till the end comes, neither denying its inevitability or becoming trapped in visions of its necessity.

I suppose this is the way I have been living, with some fraying perhaps of faith and courage around the edges. Help me to maintain that balance in the days and weeks and months ahead.

I love You.

August 15, 1995 — Grand Beach

My Love,

Mary's Day in Harvest Time — the quintessential Catholic festival, sanctifying harvest and nature and human flesh. Too bad that we don't make nearly enough of it. I will continue today my custom of giving ice cream bars to kids, a symbol of Your generosity to us in food and drink. I don't know how much of it sinks in, but they certainly like the ice cream and maybe they get the point that, like all other good things, ice cream comes from You.

Now, if You had only arranged that ice cream did not contain so many calories. Or that the new low-calorie ice cream didn't taste so much like newspaper.

But today I want to thank You again that in Your Mother role You give us life and nurse us and sustain us. Help me to keep that good news in mind as often as I can.

I love You.

August 16, 1995 — Grand Beach

My Love,

A dismal, terrible day. Mary is leaving my office for another job, a tree fell over the house in Tucson, there may be publishing conflicts, and Marilyn is sick, perhaps very seriously.

I beg You that You spare her for many more years, but I accept Your will. And I love You, You whom I know better because of her.

August 17, 1995 — Grand Beach

My Love,

Marilyn is fine, but I continue to struggle with both the loss of my administrative assistant and publishing problems.

But these are part of the difficulties of life. I have no ground for complaint.

The Cardinal is coming this afternoon for talk and supper. Talk about someone who is grace under pressure!

The Vatican has just appointed an idiot to San Francisco. All the more reason to pray that Joe recovers and lives as long as his mother!

Grant him life and health and courage. And help me to imitate a little bit of his holiness.

I love You.

August 18, 1995 — Grand Beach

My Love,

Dinner with the Cardinal last night went very well. He was in good spirits but showed fatigue when he arrived from the cumulative effect of the chemical and radiological therapies. But as the evening wore on his energies picked up. The most important information I heard from him — which hasn't made the press, I don't think — was that the tumor was caught within four weeks of its start according to blood tests only four weeks before. That should notably improve his chances. Moreover there's no sign of any recurrence so far.

He says he'll be a changed man and doubtless he will, but he is still a careful and cautious bishop, which I think is good, though some times I also find it a bit much.

He liked *White Smoke*, which is surely a good sign. Could find nothing inaccurate about it and, though he hadn't quite finished it, admitted that he had peeked to see how it ended!

He was wearing brown loafers, also a very good sign.

Again grant him as long a life as his mother has enjoyed.

I love You.

August 20, 1995 — Chicago

My Love,

I'm at the Admiral's Club at O'Hare preparing to fly to D.C. for the American Sociology Association meeting. I must remember in D.C. that I am not just a sociologist but also a priest, that I bear witness across professional lines from one to another, a bit of an outcast in both but also one who has much influence on both. In some sense when they see me they see You. Help me to be aware of that.

I love You.

August 25, 1995 — Grand Beach

My Love,

A suicide of a Grand Beach kid this week. A really nice boy who was polite and friendly and helpful to everyone. No one can understand. My guess is that he thinks he failed and let others down because of an accident with a DUI charge. Maybe his girl friend bawled him out for the accident. Part of the ordinary human condition but as a sensitive kid who expected too much of himself these events may have pushed him to despair.

No note or explanation, which means his family and friends must live with uncertainty for the rest of their lives.

You know what You're doing when You let these things happen. I don't doubt Your love either for him or for his family, but it seems so terrible, so tragic, so awful.

Help them all, I beg You. Help them to understand that You still love all of them.

How badly we have failed to preach the power and the determination of Your love. We must continue to preach it as best we can, even though the Church often seems to stand on just the opposite ground.

I love You.

August 29, 1995 — Grand Beach

My Love,

Today is the day I officially begin working on the new novels. I hope to have a draft of the Blackie book done by the end of next week and the Nuala book by the end of two weeks after that. It's a big ambition: 160,000 words in three weeks, 7,000 words a day. I figure that can be done or something reasonably close to it. I must also lose fifteen pounds during the next month. It will be a time of serious physical and intellectual discipline. I must not let my prayer life slip. No matter what happens I must do these reflections every day and my contemplative prayer (neglected during these days of guests) and perhaps on some days make it to the beach for an hour or so. That will mean bed at eight and up at four.

How do I get myself into these situations?

Some of it comes from agents. Some of it is my own fault. But it's where I am now.

I must also permit myself the right *not* to make the schedule perfectly.

I love You.

August 31, 1995 — Grand Beach

My Love,

What do you pray for, someone asked last night in our clerical bull session. I thought to myself that I pray that I might grow in my efforts to love as I am loved. It would not have fit in with what was being said, but I think it is an appropriate prayer.

I was impressed as I always am by the zeal and energy of these men. I was depressed both by the growing priest shortage, which will cause disaster in the next ten years unless something is done about it, and by their view of both the condition of the hierarchy and what will happen to Chicago if the Cardinal does not outlive the Pope as well as the condition of the clergy with so many misfits and jerks in pastoral positions.

The poor laity, I found myself thinking, they deserve so much better.

I am lucky that, without much intending it, I am on the fringes like I am. I must use this fringe position of mine to tell the truth and to try to sustain our vision through the dark days ahead. I think I will add to my prayers a fervent plea for the Church in this time of terrible suffering. It may not be much of a Church just now, but it is the only one we have.

Protect it and improve it, I beg You.

I love You. Help me to love as I am loved.

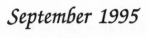

September 1995

September 1, 1995 — Grand Beach

My Love,

September 1 already!

And Labor Day weekend, which really starts tonight when everyone comes up in the massive traffic jam.

I love You. Protect everyone who is on the highway through the weekend. Protect the Church. Protect the Cardinal.

September 2, 1995 — Grand Beach

My Love,

Guests today. Not too many however. I'll try to be a good host, though.

Thirty thousand words done on the novel. Not bad for the second of September. But I must get two done this month.

They continue to be fun, and Blackie continues to preach Your love.

I wonder if official Catholic opinion will ever recognize the novels for what they are. Probably not while I'm still alive. But that's all right. So many readers do and benefit from them.

September 4, 1995, Labor Day — Grand Beach

My Love,

St. Augustine says in the passage I read this morning that instead of our finding You, You find us. True enough in my experience too, though we have at least to put aside the barriers and the obstacles because You are always ready to find us if we only open ourselves to Your love. I've learned how to do that a little better than I used to, but I still have a long way to go. There is no reason not to be open to You and Your love, especially in the next month. The trick is to translate the peace and joy I encounter with You, O my Love, into the other dimensions of my life.

I love You. Help me to love You more.

Take care of the Cardinal. Take care of the Church.

September 6, 1995 — Grand Beach

My Love,

The last guests have gone home, and I'm on a full working schedule, which means taking time off in the afternoon to go to the beach and time off in the evening to escape from the novel.

But it is very hard to escape. In the current Blackie story, I am so obsessed by the characters and their lives that they haunt me when I'm not working and especially when I try to do my contemplative prayer. You win, but it's a struggle. However, as You well know, being a story-teller Yourself, storytelling is an obsessive activity.

I find myself grieving for the young Irish servant girl whom I invented merely to record a description of Prairie Avenue in the early 1890s. She emerged as such a strong and forceful woman that I fell in love with her. Even though she survived into the early 1960s and seems to have had a happy and productive life, she still had to die. So impressive is she to me that at the end of the book Blackie will hang a picture of her in his room, along with Pope John, John Kennedy, and John Unitas.

If I am to believe the metaphor I use often of the story-teller God, You care about each of us that much. And of course I believe the metaphor, only perhaps not strongly enough. I still live and act as if I have to do it all myself, which is nonsense of course.

Help me to realize again that I too am a character in a story that an infinitely loving storyteller is making up.

I love You. Protect the Church. Protect the Cardinal.

September 7, 1995 — Grand Beach

My Love,

A bad day. I got up early to work on the novel (will finish it tomorrow) and had a three-and-a-half-hour interview with a journalist from *Time,* and now I'm waiting for some people from NBC who are doing an interview about the Cardinal and were supposed to be here an hour and a half ago. I'm dead tired already.

Too tired even to try contemplative prayer.

Too much in life.

I love You. Help the Church. Help the Cardinal.

September 8, 1995 — Grand Beach

My Love,

First novel finished, the second started. Hard work.

I love You

September 12, 1995 — Grand Beach

My Love,

I'm not doing very well this morning, as You know from watching me. Everything is going wrong. I'm tired of working on the book, tired of my fast, tired of myself, tired of life.

I don't want to go on with any of the things I'm doing. I really don't. I suppose I'll keep on trying. This is the first time in my life that I am overwhelmed by the schedule and the projects I have set for myself. Maybe it's too ambitious.

The loss of the contact lens, if it isn't still in my eye, which I doubt, was the final blow.

I'll keep trying. Help me please.

I love You. I pray for all my sick friends.

September 14, 1995 — Grand Beach

My Love,

The story is alive. I am astonished as I work on it how my imagination fashions the story, ties it together, and pushes it forward in directions I did not comprehend when I began. It will end the way I intended it to, they always do, but chance scenes which I put in almost for the fun of it become suddenly crucial to the story's twists.

I'm caught up in one of those imaginative outbursts, and the work is so compelling that it absorbs all else. I know You understand. I regret that I am not, as it were, able to spend more time with You or that when I try Nuala and Dermot and their story intrude. But I know that You are still with me and that You love me.

Thank You for the ability to tell stories. I love You. Take care of Marvin and the Cardinal.

September 17, 1995 — Grand Beach

My Love,

I have never had such a difficult time in trying to write a story and never, never, a more difficult time on Saturday. The door bell rang all day long. I had to fight to get even a paragraph written. I wonder if there is any place I can go in the world to write a book without distraction. It's a great story with lots of wonderful images and lessons. But writing it has turned into an agony of struggle.

Well, I've said that, and that's the way I feel on this early Sunday morning. I shouldn't complain. No one else can realize the agony of being pulled out of the story, so I can blame no one. I must be patient. And I have been patient. But it takes a physical toll. I should be finished soon.

I love You. Protect the Cardinal and Marvin and the Bracewells.

September 18, 1995 — Grand Beach

My Love,

Almost done. Today or tomorrow at the latest. I marvel at how a story which was at best inchoate at the beginning works itself into a coherent whole as I pound away. The agony of these days of intense work is fierce, but I'm still proud of the results. Thank You.

As I was swimming yesterday I watched Your servants the sea birds fly over the pool in neat formations, gliding on the wind drafts. It seemed obvious that they were out riding the winds for the pure fun of it. What marvelously constructed creatures they are and how proud of them You must be when You see them glide and dip and soar on a day like yesterday. Congratulations.

Joe [Cardinal Bernardin] called last night. He sounds great, so happy in his new ministry to those who are dying of cancer. What a transformation! Not a reversal, but the development of one aspect of a character that already existed. I told him that I prayed and expected that he live as long as his mother and that this experience would make him a far more effective bishop.

Please take care of him and grant him long life. I love You. Take care of Marvin too and the Bracewell family.

September 20, 1995 — Grand Beach

My Love,
    Finished!

Just in time for cold and rainy weather, which comes too early this September. Now I must go through and revise and send both of them off to the publishers.

As I revise I find that they read pretty well.

For this work and this success, much thanks. There are those who say I'm too old to work this way. I'm not at all sure why that's true. As long as I can, I should, right?

I talked to the Cardinal the other night. He sounds fine. Grant that he may flourish.

Marvin seems to be moving according to plan through his procedure.

Take care of them all.

I love You.

September 23, 1995 — Grand Beach

My Love,

Off to a Notre Dame game, an old fashioned and powerful Catholic ritual! Against the hated Longhorns. They're fun.

My editor said yesterday, in effect and very kindly, that I should have more regard for myself. She's right, of course. What really counts is Your love. As the Cardinal said yesterday on TV, we must put ourselves completely in the hands of God.

I try, but often without much effect.

The Cardinal looked great on TV. Please grant that he makes it.

I love You.

September 24, 1995 — Chicago

My Love,

Last day here. The weather turns nice! Still it's time to be home in Chicago. Thank You for the summer. Thank You for all the grace and all the love. Help me when I plunge back into the manic life in the city.

I love You.

September 25, 1995 — Grand Beach

My Love,

First full day home. Lots of running around. Not unpacked completely yet. Visited Marvin and Steve at Northwestern Hospital. Both in bad shape. What terrible places of agony hospitals are. I don't like them as You well know. No one does. I suspect that would include You. I presume I'll end up in one some day in as bad shape as anyone.

The only way to face such situations is to believe utterly and completely in Your love and that therefore all manner of things will be well.

Strengthen my faith in that outcome, I beg You.

I love You.

September 27, 1995 — Chicago

My Love,

Before I went over to the hospital this morning I read Mitch Finley's book *Whispers of Love* on contact with the dead; then on the way to the hospital I watched the little kids playing on the swings at the Eli Schumann Playground. Next I went to the hospital with all its tragedy and suffering (Please, if You can, pull Marvin through his present suffering). Finally on the evening news there was a picture of a three-year-old who had been murdered in Decatur.

What a world!

If forced to choose I'll go with the little kids in the playground. Their enthusiasms and playfulness offer the best hint of what You're like. Such is the kingdom of heaven, as Your Son said.

Mitch's interviews with people who had encounters with dead relatives or friends did not, I think, add a lot to our evidence on contact with the dead. However, they're proof of both human faith and the human will to believe, both of which in themselves are proof of something. A few of their experiences are so believable as to be almost scary.

I conclude that You have created a fascinating world, filled with all kinds of mixed signals and with sacraments lurking everywhere — in the doctors and nurses in the hospital as well as in the experiences Mitch describes and in the little kids in the playground. Not to believe in You under such circumstances takes pretty strong effort.

I must keep my eyes open to all the sacraments lurking around me and reflect on You whenever I encounter them.

I love You.

September 28, 1995 — Chicago

My Love,

Back to reading St. Augustine this morning. Still having problems. Basically he thinks the world is evil and You are the only good. I believe that the world is good, though often flawed, and that it is a sacrament of You. For all his wisdom, all his passion, and all his rhetorical skills, I find myself constantly disagreeing with him.

Thus I swam this morning, as I usually do, before I sat down for these reflections. It was an invigorating, restoring experience. I feel much better for having done it and know that it's essential that I do it every morning or at least every day. It is an aspect of this world that I pursue avidly. It is evil? Is it wrong? Does it get in the way of my love for You? Is it something I must give up because of that love?

I don't see it, not for the life of me. All right, if one is a neo-Augustinian, then the enjoyment of swimming is justified by the fact that it is necessary for my physical health, but still I must not enjoy it too much. Just as with married sex. It is tolerable if it is justified by the procreation of children, but even then one ought not to enjoy it too much. Or a beautiful woman catches my eye and I admire her beauty. Is she a creature that leads me away from You, someone from whom I must avert my eyes instantly? Or is she a sacrament of Your beauty?

In Augustine's perspective every creature distracts from You. Such distraction is tolerable only if there is some powerful excusing cause. Sacramentality is tossed out the window. Your creation is filled with intolerable evils and tolerable evils. You alone are good!

I admit that the goods of creation can be misused. But that does not make them bad. It only makes me weak. Swimming can become an obsession that distracts me from my responsibilities and commitments, though that is not likely.

Augustine was distrustful of any kind of pleasure. Human pleasures can divert us from You. But they need not. In fact they may lead us to You because they are revelations of You.

When I think how the Augustinian Neo-Platonism has infected Western Catholic spirituality, including what I was taught in the seminary, I shudder.

Well, it's on the way out.

I love You.

September 29, 1995 — Chicago

My Love,

I read another book about the 1950s yesterday, one of the worst yet. The author, currently living in Arlington, Virginia, caricaturizes his city (Chicago), his parish (St. Nicholas of Tolentine), and his later suburb (Elmhurst), and then says, well, maybe they have something that we don't have anymore — loyalty, community, respect for authority. Like for all of the so-called baby-boomers, the validity of the world in which he lives depends on the invalidity of the world of his parents — with no concern for what the world of his grandparents may have been like. Usual self-pitying nonsense!

The world has not changed all that much. There are people today who live according to the same values as did people in the 1950s, and there were people then who lived as do the rootless inhabitants of Arlington today. The proportions may have changed, but the majorities at both times are characterized by continuity rather than change — witness the high levels of marital fidelity.

He also says that most Catholics miss the stability of the 1950s Church, which is absolute nonsense.

I should write sometime about the subject, but there are so many other things to do. I don't have to engage in all the fights, do I?

I feel kind of old and tired when I read books like that. Old because I knew the 1950s and he did not. Tired because, like I say, I can't fight in every battle can I?

But maybe I'll fight in this one anyway.

Emerald Ball tonight. Help me to radiate hospitality so the ball will be a success for my guests.

I love You.

September 30, 1995 — Chicago

My Love,

I'm a bit tired this morning after the Emerald Ball last night. As always it was a lot of fun, but I didn't get to bed till 1:15, which as You know is most unlike me. Today is to be taken up with hospital visits, birthday parties, and Mass. I don't really have the energy for anything else.

I reflect on the Church's inability to consult with its most gifted people in every area. Jack Wall is one of the three most effective fund raisers in the Archdiocese. No one has ever consulted with any of them. What foolishness! If I write my book *Priests!* I will allude to that weakness. More and more I think I should write that book.

I am grateful to You that I am able to invite fifty guests to Jack's party and thus make a major contribution to the parish. It is a good work and I'm glad that I can do it and I will do it as long as I can.

Bless and protect all that were there and all that were my guests. I also thank You that I have so many nice friends.

Thanks again.

I love You.

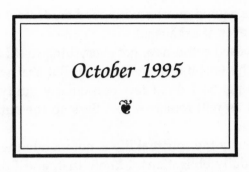

October 1995

October 9, 1995 — Chicago

My Love,

Back home in Chicago after a difficult week trying to cover the Pope for the *Today* show. It was a challenging but interesting week — Catholicism on parade and the liturgy well done. People are at last beginning to accept the communal Catholic idea. Catholics are not going to leave, but they will stay on their own terms.

I'm sorry for having lost my temper on Sunday. Travel and weariness had a lot to do with it, but still I'm sorry. I love You. Help me to love You more.

October 12, 1995 — Chicago

My Love,

Yesterday was incredibly busy. From the time I got up at seven until eleven at night I was rushing and under pressure. Even then, I did not do my interlude of contemplation or this reflection or even my daily swim. Talk about ignoring my spiritual life! The first day of class was particularly exhausting. I'd forgotten how hard it is. But it looks like a good quarter with good students. I'm sure I'll enjoy it, even if exhausted.

I suppose I could have got everything in if I did not go over to the hospital to see Marvin. But that would have been wrong. So I don't feel particularly guilty. Today is busy too as will tomorrow be. Back to the autumn rush in Chicago.

Obviously the spiritual life is not merely the execution of some daily obligations. I know that, and I don't think that's what I am doing. But if I don't schedule in my prayer (and my exercise) every day, I won't get things done. The prior question is whether I ought to live the way I do. I'm not exhausted yet, though if I go to Cologne on Thanksgiving weekend it might all catch up with me. Yet the work there is important enough that if I can go I should.

The goal should be stay somewhat ahead of the work and not fall behind it.

Help me, help me especially to realize who and what I am and who and what I should be.

I love You.

October 14, 1995 — Chicago

My Love,

Lovely Indian Summer weather swept away last night by storm, rain, and wind. I went to Navy Pier yesterday and rode Rich Daley's Ferris wheel. Great fun. Must do it again. Unlike Dermot in my novel I did not get sick.

Reading Augustine again. Why does he rub me the wrong way? Maybe because I'm so put off by this contempt for human nature. He is right that You love us beyond all our imagining. He is wrong, however, that You love us because of Yourself. Rather You love us, quite incredibly, because You find us lovable — a notion which would offend A, if he ever heard it.

We are annoying exasperating, maddening, infuriating, and, I suppose, profoundly discouraging to You. Yet You still love us. In that love our fragile dignity as human creatures is enhanced and made solid. There is no accounting for love, only accepting it and rejoicing in it. I thank You for that love which I experience sometimes in my interludes of contemplation. Grant that it may permeate my life.

October 15, 1995 — Chicago

My Love,

It has been a rough time for me since I came back from Grand Beach three weeks ago. I don't mean the time demands. I mean rather that there have been three intense personal attacks, mean, nasty, vicious. One from a friend, one from a reporter I have helped with articles, and one from a stranger. One of the accusations is that I am thin-skinned and paranoid, though the viciousness expressed would offend anyone who had the thickest of skin and create a sense of paranoia in almost anyone.

Friends say I should simply dismiss such attacks. Consider the source, they say. But that is easy advice and not good advice. I *should* listen and consider the possibility that they might be right. That is painful, but I see no alternative to it. With these there were so many gross factual errors that it was hard to imagine that there were any sound insights in them. I conclude that they made me an inkblot for their own frustrations and unhappiness — and perhaps guilt feelings. The evidence that they are wrong from other sources leaves little doubt about that.

Yet I wonder why it is necessary that I be an inkblot, why the image so many people have of me is so at odds with those of other people and of my own self-knowledge.

It goes with the territory, I guess. But it hurts. It would hurt anyone. However, You still love me and that despite the fact that You know me better than anyone else. In Your love I find my hope.

I was disheartened by the attacks, I admit, but I survive. Better now than I would have in the past.

I love You.

October 16, 1995 — Chicago

My Love,

Marvin died yesterday. They took him off the respirator. I'm sure You'll be good to him. He was, as Julie Durkin said, the world's all-time nice man. Death is no fun for anyone, is it? Not even for You.

Take care of his family.

I love You.

October 17, 1995 — Chicago

My Love,

I have taken to glance at *The Runner's Bible* each morning. Today I read a text in which You assert — courtesy of the Book of Revelation — that You are the Alpha and the Omega. And then from Jeremiah I hear Your question: "Do I not fill the heaven and the earth?'

You are indeed the Alpha and the Omega, the beginning and the end, and You do indeed fill the heaven and the earth. If You are at all, unquestionably You are those things — and a good deal more. What is harder to accept is that You love us and all the creatures with whom You have filled the cosmos (or to be precise the cosmoi), especially those creatures with whom You share the powers of knowing and loving.

Why should You love us?

I don't know, but You do, and that should be enough to ease all my worries and concerns. It isn't, but it should be. I will continue to reflect on Your power and Your love, Your ability finally to wipe away every tear and work things out so that all will be well, and indeed that all manner of things be well.

Marvin's funeral is tomorrow. I know You will take care of him as You take care of all Your children.

October 19, 1995 — Chicago

My Love,

I still feel morose and melancholy about Marvin's death. Grief but also pain at the unsatisfactory nature of the human condition. Most of what is happening now in my life seems to emphasize that unsatisfactory reality. I read in the scripture this morning that You are the one who made us stand upright, which was clever of You, even if it took millions of years. Then I see in the *Times* science section that the controversy about the Neanderthals rages on. I wonder like everyone else what happened to them. I also wonder why You permitted them to emerge and then disappear. What was the point in the Neanderthals? What was the point in all our other evolutionary ancestors? And in the terror and suffering which must have affected much of their lives — the find discussed this morning tells of signs of grief at the burial site of a child.

Why must we all die, often terribly? Some day I'll feel

an unexpected pain, or an anomaly will turn up in one of Marty's tests, or a sudden accident will occur and I will be either dead or on the way to death, most likely an embarrassing and painful one. What point in death? What point in life?

No answers to any of those questions, are there?

But I must and do believe that You loved that little Neanderthal child and that all her tears have been wiped away and she is happy. As we all will be because You love us. We will all be young again, we will all laugh again, that I most firmly believe (even if not firmly enough!). Some day perhaps I will meet that child. And certainly Marvin once again.

And I love You and ask You to deepen my love.

I append my sonnet for Marvin as a prayer and an act of faith in You:

MARVIN

A single star that broke heaven's darkling arch
A hint of dawn after a stormy night
A soft and warming wind in icy March
A smile which dissolved all unhappy blight
A shrug of shoulders and an easy grin
A lift of eyebrows and a roll of eyes
A conspiracy in which he dealt you in
And enough graceful charm to fill the skies

Spouse, father, presider at nativity
Advocate of our precious right to be free
And that parks and trees should remain the same
And Cubs, Bears, Bulls and even Notre Dame
Democrat, sweet and gentle man of peace
Witness that life is too much to ever cease.

October 20, 1995 — Chicago

My Love,

The Bible reading this morning tells me repeatedly that everything You make is good. So even a gray, glowering, gloomy day like this one is good. So in some fashion is sickness and even death. No Panglossia here, I hope. Only faith that You know what You're doing, even when it seems like You don't. Why that downpour last night when we were getting out of orchestra hall!

All right, it rained after the concert, but so what? Someone even was foolish enough to say that "we need the rain." But in fact we probably did. However the point I need to remember is that the music was so rich and lovely — three pieces inspired by Shakespeare by different composers (Berlioz, Tchaikovsky, and Elgar). If there is so much beauty, there must be Beauty.

And You're that Beauty, and I love You and all the beauty for which You are responsible. Help me to keep that in mind on this gloomy day.

October 23, 1995 — Chicago

My Love,

In the scriptures I'm reading this morning, it is asserted that You are love. I thought again about the paper I'm giving for the Illinois Humanities Council and added that metaphor to the paper. It is certain to stir up anger among any traditional Catholics who come to the session. I assert that one cannot exclude or minimize sexual love as part of the metaphor. Why has it taken us so long to realize that?

As I've said before it is a strange metaphor for You to

permit since sexual love can be so "over the top." It does not seem a decent metaphor at all. But it would seem that Your love for us, for me, is not a decent love at all. It is an overwhelming, demanding passion, one without limit or restraint. Perhaps it is the only kind of love that one can expect from the author of the Big Bang.

I continue to preach this but it is very hard to make the point with so much Jansenism still around.

I must also realize and reflect upon this truth in my own life.

I love You, help me to return Your love, You who are a demanding Lover and to whom I have responded so poorly so often.

October 28, 1995 — Chicago

My Love,

Back from my talk at the synagogue. St. Brigid visiting heaven and hell. They loved it! I really am worn out today, but I'm getting back on track after those difficult times last week.

At the synagogue this morning, during the time for meditation, I was with You again, feeling the pulse and the laughter and the joy of Your love. My contemplation flagged this week, mostly because I was so sleepy and battered. Yet I should try to find time for it every day, because it is in those moments that all my life and my effort make sense and I am captured and overwhelmed by You.

I must try to write poetry about this experience, though I'll be competing with all the mystics who wrote poetry, and I'm no Juan de la Cruz or Richard Rolle. But then I don't have to be, do I?

October 29, 1995 — Chicago

My Love,

Phil Jackson in his book *Sacred Hoops* talks about living in the moment. What wondrously sound advice. I know it to be true. I knew it all along. But I don't do that. I'm always thinking of the next thing which has to be done. Am I too old to relax?

I hope not.

I love You.

October 31, 1995 — Chicago

My Love,

It's been a disruptive morning, with crises coming up on every side, so, though I tried to begin this reflection at 8:45, I get to it only now. I certainly know how to attract trouble, don't I?

I have been reading a fascinating book about the origins of humankind. Despite all the controversy it seems pretty certain that humankind came out of Africa somewhere around two hundred thousand years ago. After millions of years of nothing much happening in the way of leaps forward, suddenly and without warning a very different kind of primate emerged. It now also appears that this new primate was not a descendent of the Neanderthal types who seem to represent an offshoot from the tree. It also seems certain that humans have a common mother — who may have been less than human herself (the Eve of the popular press), though I think she probably was.

Two big questions: (1) why did this new primate appear so suddenly without much in the way of traces of change? (2) Why did it take him/her so long before s/he began to act like we do, and why were these first humans so like the Neanderthals in their culture?

I doubt the second assumption. Because nothing has been found which indicates a different culture, it does not follow there was not one. More to the point, we are animals with a learning curve. It probably took a long time for us to catch on to things. Thus the breakthrough perhaps thirty or forty thousand years ago was the result of tens of thousands of years of accumulated knowledge and culture.

The first question is more puzzling. One of the scientists in the book admits frankly that we don't know why this new primate appeared. I accept the assumption that it emerged out of some kind of evolutionary development. But it was a rapid and, considering the long time, our ancestors were around, a surprising one.

One of Your neat tricks, I suspect. Using the evolutionary process to show up what You can do!

It is now 7:21 at night. A *very* busy day. Again. And school tomorrow. Anyway I wanted to say by way of ending that I am impressed with the creature that finally emerged from the evolutionary "soup." You have made him/her, as the Psalmist says, "a little less than the angels." A lot less it seems sometimes. We have so much to learn. Help us on the way.

I love You.

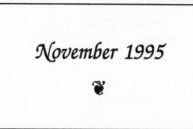

November 1995

November 1, 1995 — Chicago

My Love,

Busy day. Class is so much hard work with many of the young people not responsive. That's their problem, but it makes it hard. They seem to like the course, but they want to sit there and be passive.

I talked about saints on this feast of all saints, how to sort out the superstition and folk religion from faith and orthodoxy — and the tolerance to see the overlap that is inevitable. They seem interested. Then we talked about Protestant folk religion in the Rapture cult.

I reflect after the class what an incredible variety humankind has devised to relate to You. I suspect some of them You don't like very much. But in many of them are authentic revelations of You. Once You produced a creative and imaginative creature like this advanced primate homo sapiens sapiens You must have known that You would get this variety, everything from mystic experience to human sacrifice. Everything from slavery to the civil rights movement, everything from ritual prostitution to Poor Clares.

Maybe because I'm tried today, it all kind of over-

whelms me. Someone (Ingrid I think) said that the Catholic metaphor system is a rain forest of imagery. So is
human religion a rain forest. I hope I have persuaded the
students of that.

Anyway, it is both fun and exhausting.

I love You.

November 2, 1995 — Chicago

My Love,

I want to make it clear first of all that You are within
Your rights in doing things the way You do them — in
setting up, for example, the quantum puzzle and direct-
ing (one way or another) the human evolutionary process
the way You did. You are certainly within Your rights in
launching everything with a Big Bang. These processes
baffle us, but any God who did not baffle us would not be
much of a God.

My problem this morning is how to reconcile these
awesome and mind-boggling enterprises with Your concern for us as individuals. This is of course the Deist
problem. Why should You care? The Deists are wrong,
I think, because what kind of a God would it be that
wouldn't care about Her children. However, their point
is well taken. Why should a Reality so enormous and so
powerful and so clever bother with creatures at all?

This is something like Nuala McGrail's problem in
my novels about her. Not whether You would love Your
creatures, but why make them in the first place.

An unanswerable question, obviously.

I encounter You in my efforts, however inept, at contemplation in the morning. I think to myself, this is the
One who made the Big Bang. Obviously I am encoun-

tering You in the "fine point" of my being where You left Your trace. But it's still You and the fine point is there because You chose to make us creatures who could encounter it.

Beats me. You must love me, all of us, everyone something fierce. I believe that but it still is a shattering truth that I have not even begun to absorb.

I love You.

November 6, 1995 — Chicago

My Love,

The death of Prime Minister Rabin over the weekend reveals again how fragile all things human are. Chance, to say nothing of malice, can undo the best and most generous and most loving hopes of humans. A family bereft because of a drunken driver or a gang banger, a hardworking man deprived of his job by corporate greed, a love destroyed by a miscue, thousands dead because of a storm, high school kids killed by a faulty signal crossing — all these are random events which seem to have no reasonable, no possible explanation. The Israelis we are told are angry at Rabin's death. Big deal! What good does anger do? At whom to be angry? The killer? But he is hardly worth the anger. The extremists? But the extremists have their own political agenda. Anger doesn't do any good, though we are all angered at loss and look for someone to strike out at — Arab Americans at the time of the Oklahoma City blast or an innocent sibling when a parent dies. Or a friend who happens to be an available target (tell me about it!).

It's the fragility of our own dreams, our own hopes, our own joys which angers us.

Appropriate thoughts, are they not, when I am about to go to the doctor? I pray that all will be well, but I know that such need not be the case at all.

No matter what, I love You.

November 7, 1995 — Chicago

My Love,

I was fine yesterday, but my doctor was in bad shape. Broken hand and woozy from pain killers. Poor man. Please take care of him.

And thank You again for the astonishing good health I seem to have, most of it genetic "luck," some of it, I suppose, the result of my lifestyle — no smoking, exercise, little booze, etc. Help me to make good use of the health You have given me in Your service and the service of Your kingdom.

I love You. Help me to love You more.

November 9, 1995 — Chicago

My Love,

The Cardinal stopped by. He looked very frail, though he seemed vigorous. The once-a-week dose of chemicals is getting to him, poor man. He worries, as anyone must, about the future of the Church and of the Archdiocese. There are so many bad people out their threatening the Church. The drive to undo in fact if not in theory the Second Vatican Council goes on. Again I pray for him and for all of us. And I thank You for the grace of reconciliation with which we have been blessed.

I love You.

November 13, 1995 — Chicago

My Love,

I reflect this morning on Bob Barron's comment in his book *Thomas Aquinas* on the difference between Your love for us and human passion. The metaphor errs, I'm fond of saying, by defect, not by excess. You are more passionate than the most passionate of human lovers. However, unlike human lovers, even the best of them, You do not waver or vary or give in to moods or become inconsistent or inconstant or become frightened and pull back. Your love, I have often said, is implacable. It never turns away, never hesitates, never gets fed up.

That must be difficult. I mean, You're God and You can do things that we can't do. But either Your patience is so far beyond ours that we cannot imagine it or it is sometimes sorely tested. Or maybe both.

Anyway You are ecstasy and I must believe that with all my heart and mind and I must learn to believe it a little more each day. Help me to do so on this important day of my life.

November 15, 1995 — Chicago

My Love,

My day of recollection on Monday went reasonably well, despite interruptions, including one at the end of the day which resolved a major problem. For that I am very grateful.

One conclusion from the day of recollection: how quickly I forget humility and the purposes of my activities when I am swept up by worry and trouble. I began to write books and still write them to spread Your good news. The problems surrounding them cause me to become so immersed in the economic and financial and administrative problems that I forget why I write the books and what they're about. It's very hard to keep the ego distinct from my goals when I am caught up in such difficulties. I must try harder and must rely more on Your love, which I experience almost physically in my contemplative prayer. At least yesterday when I was running around with lunch, tea, and supper, plus the beginning of Christmas shopping, I was able to remember You and Your love often. Help me to continue to do so, I beg You.

And so to mean it when I say that I love You.

November 18, 1995 — Chicago

My Love,

Five weeks to Christmas and I've already put up the tree and arrayed my vast number of crib scenes. I have Christmas music playing on the stereo and I'm bringing Christmas disks down to the car this afternoon. I'm not the only one. The Merchandise Mart is already bathed in red and green lights and so is the Hancock Center. That's rushing things I guess. Still in the dark of mid-November it's nice to have a promise of light. More to the point, I'll be away from Wednesday to Monday, first at Grand Beach and then at Cologne, so it's do it this weekend or not get to it for another three weeks.

The *Messiah* is playing now: make the crooked straight and the rough places plain. Not a bad idea!

I feel much better than I usually do at this time of the year, for any number of reasons, not the least of which is my contemplative prayer. It may just be remaking my life, for which many thanks. I am terribly distracted during that prayer, even when I choose time during which the phone is not supposed to ring. Help me to get better at cleansing the distractions from my mind.

I don't want to be swept up by exhaustion during the Christmas weeks. Help me to be a source of joy and light to others.

I love You.

November 19, 1995 — Chicago

My Love,

The lights of Chicago went on last night, defying darkness just as our distant ancestors defied it. I rejoice in the return of the light only a month and two days away. I rejoice in the lights on the Magnificent Mile just below me — and on Navy Pier this year. I rejoice because they remind me that light came into the world once and again and always. Your light came with creation, it came with special radiance at Bethlehem, it comes with every birth of a new child (even the poor kid who was torn from his dead mother's womb by her killer the other day out in Addison; help the poor kid, he'll need it), it comes with every rededication of a human person, every rebirth of love, every renewal of commitment.

As I walk down the street of lights and listen to the carols, help me to reflect especially on Your light within me and to radiate that light in joy and peace and not cloud it with anger and impatience this Christmas season.

I love You.

November 20, 1995 — Chicago

My Love,

You sent Your Son to be the light of the world and the way, the truth, and the life and that we might have life and have it more abundantly. I cannot help but reflect today about how badly the Church carries that message, how terribly it has failed, how much it has turned the good news into bad news — all in Your name of course!

The Church helped the Communists win the Polish election yesterday. It has messed up the situation in Ireland. The Holy Office, which has no authority to do so, has ruled the Pope's letter on women priests as "infallible." All of these actions are unrelated to the Good News and indeed are merely efforts by the institutional bureaucracy to hang on to its own power over the lives of Your people. It does not try to attract; rather it tries to compel, to constrain, to force. How ugly!

None of this means that the heritage is wrong. It only means that the Church desperately needs reform — and is resisting it now as fervently as it can. I will do whatever little I can do to promote reform, though it is more important that I preach the good news, especially through my stories.

I am not all that good a priest myself. I did not lose my temper at the woman next to me at the football game yesterday, though she pushed and kicked and elbowed me and leaned over half my seat area. If I had not thought yesterday morning about losing my temper and begged You that I would not do so, I'm afraid I would have blown up at her. I didn't, but like I say my reaction was not very Christian, even if I did hold it back. Better perhaps if I had asked her not to push me, though that would have been a waste of time too. How does one handle such matters?

I have two ways, one is to repress anger and the other is to blow up. Neither of them is very good, but the first is better, and I am grateful to You that I didn't blow up yesterday. I don't know.

Yet I am still the light of the world, as are all of us. Help my light to shine more freely, more radiantly, especially during these tough two weeks that lie ahead of me.

I love You.

November 24, 1995 — A half hour out of Düsseldorf

My Love,

Thanksgiving was fun yesterday. I hated to leave and hated even more to ride up to the airport and get on this plane. However, I did manage to finish most of the minor revisions on *White Smoke* at the airport and on the plane, which is a big load off my mind.

I ask how I got myself into this project at my age in life.

The answer is that age has nothing to do with it as long as health holds, and my health seems to be holding. Help me to perform well here and to represent You and the Church well despite my weariness.

I love You. Help me to love You more.

Again many thanks for the good day yesterday.

November 25, 1995 — Cologne

My Love,

The sun was out almost all day and this beautiful city was simply gorgeous. More and more do I like it. I slept through two alarms this morning but managed to make it for the beginning of the meeting, which was quite good, though overwhelming because there is so much that we want to do. The group was open to my ideas on religious imagery, which is a change from other groups. There was also a very good review of my book *Religion as Poetry* in the *Journal for the Scientific Study of Religion* which surprised and pleased me. Could it be possible that the ideas I have worked on so long are at last becoming accepted. If that be true, I'm very grateful to You.

Also I am grateful for my relationship with the people here and the way it has brought me into the international community studying sociology of religion. Better late than never.

I must in this sociological context continue to emphasize the religious experience of ordinary people.

I love You.

November 26, 1995 — Cologne

My Love,

The meeting is over. I'm going home tomorrow. Good meeting as meetings go.

Rather late in life for me to have become an international expert in the sociology of religion. Mostly the result, I suspect, of having written a lot and made a lot of noise.

But I am grateful, at the risk of repeating myself, for the good friends I have made here. At whatever time in life, they are good friends and I am fortunate to have them.

This is all a great adventure. But then that's what life is, is it not? A great adventure, a marvelous opportunity, a wonderful chance. Help me to live as though I believe that is true, to savor the excitement, to revel in the opportunity, to enjoy the adventure.

I love You, You who has orchestrated the adventure.

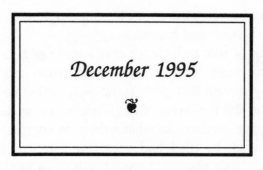

December 1995

December 1, 1995 — Chicago

My Love,

Chicago Symphony last night. I was pretty sleepy, as I usually am. But Mahler's 8th was a profoundly moving experience — a bitter, sardonic, ultimately sad composition of a man dying young after the death of a daughter and with a young and beautiful wife (the legendary Alma) to leave behind. In a sense the symphony is an indictment of You and life and fate from one who had reason to be angry.

He did not know when he died shortly after the performance of this piece whether his music would be accepted or not. Finally it is accepted and lavishly praised. I decided, as I was listening last night, that he is almost certainly the greatest composer of the twentieth century.

What good does it do him now?

My faith says that he enjoys it in You and with You, You who also rejoice every time a child of Yours is celebrated for the use of the talents You bestowed upon him.

But one uses talents as best one can without expectation of celebration but because they are given to be used and in the using of them there is joy and peace. Anything else must be accepted as a pleasant surprise in a world filled with envy and hatred.

I think of this as I glance over *Angel Light*, to be published this week. There is so much spiritual good in it as in all my novels that goes completely unnoticed by the critics and the reviewers, though not by the readers.

So I have readers, so what's there to complain about? Mahler when he died had very few listeners. But even if I didn't have readers, I would still revel in the fun of putting stories together.

I love You.

December 12, 1995 — Chicago

My Love,

As I was sitting in the dentist's chair yesterday, I gazed out the window at the strange and compelling view of tall buildings, alleys, and darkening sky with wisps of smoke, thick in the cold, creeping up to the sky in ever changing patterns. A chaos system, I suppose. I marveled at the beauty of the scene and the variety of the smoke and thought of You and how clever You have been to produce such a wonder, which I may have been the only one to notice.

Do You feel upset when people don't notice Your work? Or are You happy that the beauty, which reflects Your beauty, is out there?

Anyway I thought of Your beauty, Your goodness, and Your love and wished that I had the time to think more about that during this Christmas season, which somehow seems more crowded than most. Maybe Saturday I will get a chance to recollect.

Help me to see You every day in the ordinary and extraordinary events of my life.

I love You.

December 16, 1995 — Chicago

My Love,
   A few haiku for Christmas time:

> *In the fog and rain*
> *On the top of tall buildings*
> *Dim red and green glow*

> *A winter sunrise*
> *Over the quiet city*
> *The fog fades away*

> *On a skyscraper*
> *Between two TV towers*
> *Star of Bethlehem*

> *Sheet ice on the lake*
> *Long shadows from tall buildings*
> *Aquamarine sky*

> *Soft carol music*
> *Red and green tissue paper*
> *Stacks of Christmas gifts*

> *Gray clouds hover low*
> *anxious hurrying shoppers*
> *At last Christmas eve*

December 25, 1995 — Chicago

A little more daylight
Shapeless plumes of frozen smoke
Christmas day is here

December 27, 1995 — Chicago

My Love,

It's been a rough Christmas. I continue to rush. and when I tried to slow down on Christmas eve I couldn't. Then it seemed to be a time when a lot of people wanted to beat up on me, perhaps taking out their Christmas resentments. All of it was without objective reason. I guess I was an inkblot again. I understand where the anger is coming from and why. Yet it still hurts. Last night it kept me from sleeping.

I can absorb this stuff if I have to, and patently I have to, but I don't like it and cannot be expected to like it, can I?

Anyway I love You. I know that You don't have to erupt at me, which is reassuring.

December 28, 1995 — Chicago

My Love,

This is a season of love manifest, the most powerful manifestation of Your love the world has ever witnessed. As one of my e-mail correspondents said the other day, we are all so much better than we think we are. At least we are good enough to be loved unconditionally by You, which is no small feat. Why am I rushing like crazy at this time of the year?

Beats me!

A couple of phone interruptions since the last paragraph!

Oddly enough I'm not exhausted like I often am at this time of the year. Just pushed.

Anyway, You do love us and love us a lot, which is odd but wonderful. As I said in the proposal for *The Book of Love*, to be is to be desirable and desired, by You especially, but by lots of others too. I hope You like the proposal. I don't think it will fly both because it is so different and because it is so Catholic. But it's a good idea.

I love You. Help me to love You more and show Your love to others by the way I live.

Author's Note

Two bad things happened in the interim between these reflections.

First, I bought a new computer, a Compaq 5300. It was not a lemon but a lemon grove. The company, arrogant with its success, refused even to answer my letters of complaint — though I must have bought twenty of their products over the years. So far they have installed four new system boards, two new processors, and three new power supplies. It works now, more or less, but it still won't function on battery power. Caveat emptor.

One of its early crimes was to eat the missing reflections. They are in the mind of God, Herself be praised, but no longer on my hard disk or my backups.

The other bad thing was a bout of illness which seemed very serious but in fact was not. Scary though. Coming home in the evening of Paddy's Day, I sat down at the computer and wondered if it would work. It did, but I didn't.

I began to bleed internally. Copiously. Sunday night, my

M.D. in Chicago wasn't home. So I left a message for him, made an airline reservation for a flight to Chicago, finished my work, and went to bed.

There was so much blood I thought I was going to die. (In fact, I lost half my red blood cells.) Strangely enough I faced that truth with something like relief. The struggle was over, I thought.

Perhaps if the bleeding had continued, I would have gone through the other Kübler-Ross stages.

Marty Phee met me at Little Company of Mary Hospital, with, would You believe, a suite. By the end of the day there was a diagnosis — ruptured diverticulum. Usually nature seals up the wound, I was told. It did. So thanks be to God I didn't need surgery. The Cardinal, God be good to him, came to see me, as did lots of other folk. I wasn't able to get much work done on my laptop, which of course I brought along. Roberta, my administrative assistant, drove me home on Friday. I was anemic for a couple of months and worn out till the autumn.

What did I learn from the experience:

(a) I can no longer eat popcorn.

(b) I can face the thought of my own death.

March 28, 1996 — Tucson

My Love,

It's been eight days since my last attack of bleeding, so I guess I'm free of it. At least I hope so. And I pray You that it be so. I'm still very weak and dragged out. But I am still alive. Not much energy. Or at least not my accustomed energy. Again I thank You for my recovery. I ask You to help me to understand what lessons are to be learned from the incident. I told Doug last night that I worked on an article while flying to Chicago despite the fact that I had bled copiously before I left for the airport. He thought that remarkable, or perhaps I should say odd. I remembered the story about St. Aloysius who said he would keep playing billiards, though I did not retell the story.

Did I think I was going to die? I certainly thought I might. I made a phone call the night before which seemed to imply that. Yet I went right on with my work. Was that good or bad? I don't know, but it's what I did and what I would do again. I don't say that I was not afraid to die or even that I was ready to die, but that I was accepting of the possibility. I'm not going to get cocky about that; I'm merely thanking You for the grace.

The reading today has You wondering why I don't know You when You are closer to me than I am to myself. Fair question.

Back to contemplation this afternoon.

I love You.

March 30, 1996 — Tucson

My Love,

I'm not doing very well. I have a cold and am still weak from my interlude in the hospital last week. Moreover I don't think I have recovered psychologically or emotionally from what happened. Maybe it's all physiological. Maybe when I rout the cold and my blood count goes up I will feel better. But just now I am devoid of energy and confidence and hope.

Moreover, it's harder than ever to pray. That despite the lovely weather and the blue sky and the beginning of spring and the fact that April is almost upon us. I'll snap out of all of this, I know. However today I want to reassert that I love You and that I know You love me. Maybe I should try to make a bit of a retreat tomorrow, Palm Sunday. I have nothing on my schedule. I could at least try for a day of recollection.

I thank You for my life and that I did not die as I thought I would two weeks ago. Help me to make good use of my life. I love You.

March 31, 1996 — Tucson

My Love,

Two weeks now from my "attack." I talked to Jack [Shea] this morning about the way I felt that night. He quoted a wonderful Sufi line: Better to die in the morning than to die at night. Which I take to mean that it's better to accept death when your acceptance still means something more than just a bowing to the inevitable.

To be perfectly honest about it, I thought I would very likely die from the bleeding. What did I feel? Relief. I hesitate to write that, even to think it. But that's the way I felt. One had to die some time. One might just as well do it now and get it over with. All the weariness, all the controversy, all the demands would be over. So I finished the article I was working on, made a phone call, and went to bed. No raging against the failing of the light.

Then in the middle of the night the call to the airline and packing for the trip. Then the flight to Chicago.

By day's end I knew that this was not the time.

But I wasn't terrified or resentful or angry. Or even afraid of dying. The sight of all that blood was scary, but I was not afraid.

I don't know how weird any of this is. Jack thinks it's healthy or at least more healthy than not. Well, that last sentence is my modification of his comment. I'm sure that a lot of fear would have happened later on if I was really dying. But I don't think the sense of relief would have gone away.

Strange. A grace maybe. Maybe too fatalistic. Or maybe just that I didn't have a family which would suffer the way a spouse and children suffer.

I don't know for sure what any of this means, but I do incline to think that You have blessed me in this matter of life and death and I am grateful.

My organism, however, has not caught up. It's tired and uneasy. I'll have to give it time.

I am terribly weak, but I think I am getting better.

I love You.

April 1, 1996 — Tucson

My Love,

Holy week begins. I want to make it a good Holy Week,
and I beg You for Your help. However, I have a bad cold, I
am week from the attack last week, and I must pack to go
home. Also I continue to have computer problems.

Other than that I guess everything is okay.

Also the birds are going wild and waking me up in the
morning.

Well, I'm going to try. I love You. Help me to love
You more.

April 3, 1996, Wednesday in Holy Week — Tucson

My Love,

So, okay, I accept the present frailty and will not complain against it. I offer up to You my flawed and imperfect
Holy Week and my humiliation because of it. I know You
love me regardless of how well I respond to the liturgical
year or how well I pray. I understand as today's reading
tells me that while sky and earth cannot contain You, You

81

are nonetheless contained entirely on the heart of the one who adores You.

Even when the adoration is imperfect and distracted and frail and tired.

So I adore You on this Wednesday in Holy Week.

April 4, 1996, Holy Thursday — Tucson

My Love,

Well, the Tucson interlude ends in ignominy. I am returning to Chicago this afternoon, two days early, because of acute dental problems. I miss the Holy Thursday services and my class tomorrow. I feel yucky.

However, I guess I must accept this whole mess as being part of the human condition and, yes, part of getting old, and accept it cheerfully, even though I feel guilty about the class and sad about the liturgy tonight.

Paradoxically, I think I'm getting my strength and energy back, for which I am very grateful. I presume this more abrupt transition will be hard. I must strive to be cheerful and pleasant.

I love You. I accept all that happens as part of Your will for me. Help me to love You more.

April 6, 1996, Holy Saturday — Chicago

My Love,

I went to the Good Friday services at old St. Patrick's last night. Very impressive. John Cusick preached on the persistence of death and evil in the world and how Good Friday and Easter are signs of how You respond. You do not deny death; rather You die with us. Easter is built into Your nature.

Your Son made the covers of both *Time* and *Newsweek* this week, giving more publicity to the Jesus Seminar and other skeptics, even though both articles came down solidly on the side of Jesus, which was nice of them. They miss the point that our faith in the resurrection is not in a physical phenomenon but rather in Your love as manifested in the risen Jesus. You are the only proper object of faith. I do believe in You and Your personal love for me and that, just as I live in You, I will, when it comes time to die, die in You.

I still am feeling very fragile, as my M.D. says I will continue to feel. My dreams and my passing images very much emphasize frailty.

As well they should, for I am a frail being, existing in the palm of Your hand. I accept that frailty (I didn't say I liked it!) and will live in confidence and trust as best I can for however many years You give me.

I believe in Your love as manifested in the risen Jesus. I love You as best I can in return.

April 7, 1996, Easter Sunday — Chicago

My Love,

The festival is about life, about resurrection, and I'm having a hard time tuning into it because of all the new demands and problems. Help me, I beg of You.

I believe that Your Son rose from the dead, and more specifically I believe in Your love which was revealed in that triumph over death. I'm sorry I don't feel that way. But faith is not a matter of feeling.

Anyway I love You. Help me to radiate that love today.

April 10, 1996 — Chicago

My Love,

Reasonably good news from the doctor yesterday: my blood count is up to 10 which is a lot better than 8.7, though still only "two-thirds" of the way to normal. So I am getting better, somewhat slowly but still at a rate which he found more than satisfactory. So three weeks after the end of the bleeding, I mend. It was a devastating trauma, but, thank You, not fatal. I also thank You for the recovery and the general improvement of my health — even though it is still very difficult to get up in the morning.

In my reading today it is said that no one can gaze directly at the sun, but they can see the reflected light in the water. So no one can see You directly but we can see You as You are reflected in creation.

This time of the year, as nature struggles to come to life and as the naked city searches for its clothes, I see especially Your reflection. Despite the cold, despite the long winter, despite the melancholy of the citizenry, spring forces its way into being. The grass does not so much become green as a little less brown, the day is a little longer, life lurks just beneath the surface.

A small change of seasons on a small planet in a small galaxy, and yet here there is a hint of the Lord of Creation, of You, of Your love, and of Your implacable commitment to life and indeed to superabundant life.

In my own slow recovery from serious illness and despite the failing of vigor which comes from age, I sense the same stirrings of superabundant life. And with that I also feel hints of love, of Your love, love which is always in springtime.

I love You. Help me to love You more.

April 11, 1996 — Chicago

My Love,

Today I reflect on Suso's comparison of You with a wild flower. You spring up in places where we least expect You. You dazzle us with Your color. You blow away when we try to pick You and make You our own. And when we try to stamp You out, You come back to life again.

I see wild flowers along the roadside in Michigan and in my own garden in Tucson or in the median strip — not so many this year. (Suso could have added that like the wild flowers You seem to come and go.) What can I say of them? They are casual and gratuitous beauty. They don't have to be there, but they are, as if someone in a wild moment of prodigality spread them out for our temporary and passing amusement. I do not make enough of them. I don't stop and admire them. I don't give You thanks for them. I hurry on with my schedule, catching them out of the corner of my eye.

Like so much other beauty that reflects You.

I am sorry for this neglect, sorry that I rush pell-mell through life as I must today. Sorry that I don't spend more time exulting in spring coming to life in my city (we can do without the snow promised for next Monday if You don't mind!).

Help me always to think of You when I see the wild flowers — or the not so wild flowers in my garden at Grand Beach.

I love You, O Beauty, ever ancient, ever new.

April 12, 1996 — Chicago

My Love,

"Love is an infinite sea whose skies are a bubble of foam. Know that it is the waves of love that turn the wheels of heaven." Thus Rumi in today's reading. Or to put it a little less metaphorically, that energy and power which animates the universe is best represented in our existence by the human emotion we call love.

Powerful stuff. I believe it. I wish to live by it. But on a foggy day when I have been to the dentist and must go twice next week, when I'm running around and catching up, when I must dash out to the university, when I must make plans for my trip to Milan and Slovenia, when I am waiting for the Gallup data, when I must catch up on my mystery story, when I must analyze more data for my Ireland paper, it's hard to keep that in mind, it's hard to realize that love is grinding away — no, that's the wrong word, spinning away, whirling away, exploding away, and thus keeping everything going.

It is difficult to realize that I live on a sea of love which is embracing me with warmth and power and light.

Nonetheless that's where I live. Help me to bask, relax, give myself over to that love, especially tomorrow, which I intend to be a day of recollection.

Help me to realize that Your love is absolutely implacable.

April 16, 1996 — Chicago

My Love,

I read in three separate passages this morning (Thomas à Kempis, Bonaventure, and a Parsee) that You are light flooding the world. I believe that. Darkness is retreating now (the sun is out in Chicago, astonishingly enough), and it's wonderful.

Thank You for all the light and for being Light.

I am still dragging. I wonder if I'm more tired this week than last week. Well, I'll get over it in Your own good time. Protect me on the trip to Kentucky.

I love You.

April 18, 1996 — Chicago

My Love,

Back from Kentucky. Talk went well. Bishop there is great. I was really worn out and still am. However my blood count is up to 10.5, which is a good sign.

I talked to the Cardinal. Still no sign of cancer. Back is better because of a new brace. Grant him life and health.

This afternoon I feel like I'm running in a swamp, making no progress at all against all the demands of the day and of my different conflicting roles, or at least different roles, all demanding my time.

Excuse me for running. I love You.

April 21, 1996 — Chicago

My Love,

Well, the computer erased without warning my first comments on the emotions I felt upon returning to Christ the King today to celebrate the Eucharist. A couple of times I was so moved that I almost wept. The place is a little shabby from time, and, as Joe says, there's a lot of work that needs to be done. But in most respects it's a better parish than it was when I was there as an assistant pastor so many years ago. Many people I knew in the old days were there at Mass, looking older (of course I don't look older!) and many children and grandchildren. The deacon was a man whose grandmother I had taken care of my first year there. I remembered the name and the house.

Oh, dear God, the memories, memories, memories. So many ghosts, so many demons, so much love.

And so much gratitude to You for that unending formative experience of my life. It's still my neighborhood. I love it so much. Thank You for giving me the opportunity to go back.

I wonder if they will want me back again. I hope so.

I love You, and today I am very grateful.

April 24, 1996 — Chicago

My Love,

Once one becomes impassioned with God, my morning reading tells me, everything else falls into place.

Even anemia, even getting up in the morning, even preparing for a trip to Slovenia? Gimme a break!

On the subject of anemia, my red cells are at 11.5 and they should be at 15. I have a long way to go before I recapture my energy. Clearly I am leaving for Portoroz without nearly enough of it. Maybe not a good idea. Still the doctor says it's all right.

As I've said to You before, I accept the weariness which comes from my anemia as part of the human condition. I will not complain about it. I wish only that I could go to Grand Beach now and do nothing.

I love You.

April 25, 1996 — Chicago

My Love,

Really wiped out this morning. No energy at all. Offer it up. What else can I do!

I love You.

April 26, 1996 — Chicago

My Love,

Better today. Not a lot but some. Maybe the tonic I'm taking is a help. Still struggling through the swamp. I hope I turn around while I'm away on the trip.

I love You.

April 28, 1996 — Chicago

My Love,

I'm at O'Hare getting ready for the trip to Milano and Portoroz. I feel pretty good, mostly because I had a nap before leaving. I ask You to protect me and take care of me on this trip. Grant that my full health and energy and wit may return as the trip progresses. Also grant that my conversation with Cardinal Martini goes well tomorrow. Also protect my own Cardinal who is going to Rome to show them that he's still alive and kicking. "I'm in good health," he said to me today on the phone. A gutsy observation.

As You well know I love to travel and hate to travel. I love new places and new people and don't have any of the bodily systems which make for a good traveler. At least help me to be patient and radiate Your love to all I encounter. I love You.

April 29, 1996 — Milano

My Love,

We're about a half hour out of Milano. Not a bad crossing. Crowded plane. No upgrade to first class. Pilot didn't tell us the Bulls score. Nine more nights away from home.

Help me to relax and even enjoy this trip, while, as I always do, I count the days and the hours till I return home.

I love You.

April 30, 1996 — Milano

My Love,

Very fine lunch with Cardinal Martini yesterday. What a warm, witty, and wise man he is — and very much a moderate in Church affairs. He would truly make a great Pope. He agrees with my thesis that pluralism is the issue in the next election. He also says that he reads my novels, in part, for the humor in them. That was very nice. There's a lot of humor in the stories, but almost no one ever notices or comments. And English is not his first language!

He wants to read *White Smoke* and says that, like Joe, he will peek at the end to see if the good guy wins. I'll send him the book of course. I hope he is not offended by it.

I love You.

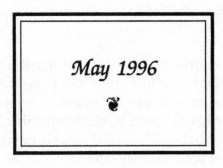

May 1996

May 4, 1996 — Portoroz (Port of the Roses)

My Love,

It is a totally gorgeous day here on the Slovenian Litoral. Breathtaking.

One of the other sociologists asked Niko last night when Slovenia first became free. He said 1990. They said no, in the past. His reply was that this country was never a country till 1990. They are mighty proud of their new country and not without serious reason. I suspect it is an effort to display the greatness of their little country of two and a half million people that they have laid on this great event for us. As I tell people, I don't want to work. The work actually won't begin till tomorrow, and I think I'll duck a lot of it.

Tomorrow is my forty-second anniversary as a priest. I've celebrated the day in some odd places, have I not — the Galway mountains, Budapest, Fiesoli, now here in Slovenia.

I thank You for the excitement and the adventure of the last forty-two years, and I ask for Your help in responding ever better to Your love in whatever years are ahead.

I love You.

May 6, 1996 — Portoroz

My Love,

The days at the ISSP [International Social Science Program] wind down. Mike and I had a good day winning support for a number of good causes — especially on getting the Pope study done in other countries. It is already going out in Spain. This should be a big help to the whole project. I lost patience only once.

I'm leaving early tomorrow to go to Milano tomorrow night so I won't have to get up at 4:00 A.M.

I love You.

Protect me on the way home.

May 8, 1996 — Over Europe

My Love,

Heading home at last. Nice trip, all things considered. I think my health has notably improved. At least mornings are not as bad as they have been. Probably a way to go yet.

My sister Grace is sick. Grant her recovery. I'll try to see her soon. Also grant eternal peace and joy to Teri's mother and family.

Thank You for the graces and protection of this trip.

I love You.

May 9, 1996 — Chicago

My Love,

Back home, thank You. Blood count up to 12.6 so I'm getting there. Thank You very much. I'm busy getting organized. Nice to be home, even if it was a good trip.

I love You.

May 11, 1996 — Chicago

My Love,

I corrected the papers from my class in Arizona yesterday. What nice young people. How impressive their religious search, how grateful for my class (as imperfect and shortened as it was), how concerned about my health.

I feel that I'm the lucky one to have known them. I regret that circumstances made it impossible for me to get to know them better. But nothing could be done about that.

I love You.

May 12, 1996 — Chicago

My Love,

I'm off to the hospital in another hour to see my sister Grace, who (for which many thanks to You) apparently does not have stomach cancer.

God is not always silent, says my late friend Rabbi Heschel in this morning's reading. Sometimes the veil is lifted and one gets a hint of the beauty, peace, and power which flow through the souls of those who are devoted to God.

Absolutely true. I have had such experiences and I know that You are not always silent, that indeed You are not really a hidden God at all. To the extent we think of You as hidden, the reason is that we can't bear the sight of the unhidden God.

Right now I'm so sleepy that I can only long for You as You reveal Yourself in my interludes of contemplation. But I'm going to keep trying.

Help me.

I love You.

May 14, 1996 — Chicago

My Love,

I saw the doctor yesterday and he pronounces me in good condition but adds that it will take six more weeks to get over the effect of the hemorrhage. Tells me that I lost about half my blood. Wow!

I am not seriously sick. I will get better. Those who are seriously sick and will not get better have a much harder time during this season of life than I do. I do not complain. I ask merely for Your tolerance, which I know I have already and have had for a long time.

I love You. Help me to love You more.

May 16, 1996 — Grand Beach

My Love,

The single light over the entrance to Grand Beach is powerful when you are under it, but dim and forlorn in the distance. Yet it is a welcome light to me, a beacon of hope and peace. I do slow down up here, not enough, especially when the rush of summer is on me. But at least some. I am terribly unhappy about Tucson this year, though most of the problem was health. I don't want to mess this opportunity up. Help me every time I enter the village to understand why You put it in my life: more than any of the other reasons (and they were good) is that I might find more time for You.

There are still ghosts haunting this place, ghosts of lost opportunities and shattered relationships, of animosity and ambivalence. These ghosts are pale and faint, lost in great part in the mists of the past. There's nothing that can be done about any of them, except to learn from my mistakes, which I think I have at least in part.

Nonetheless, those failures were not what You had in mind when You put this house in my life. Help me to realize the potential in my relationship with You of this time up here.

I love You.

May 19, 1996 — Grand Beach

My Love,

The Mass at Christ the King this morning was wonderful again. So many memories, not all of them good, but the memories the people have of me are good and the kids like my Mass, which is reassuring because they are not working out of memories.

I'll be back there next month. And of course continuing to say Mass at St. Mary of the Woods. From having no parishes in Chicago I now have two! For which many thanks to You.

As You can tell, I'm upbeat.

And I love You.

May 20, 1996 — Grand Beach

My Love,

The tree that overhangs my pool was barren on Saturday when I swam for the first time. Yesterday when I came back it was budding. This morning it was almost in bloom. Thus does 90-degree sunshine affect nature. A kiss of love, if one wishes. Warmth calling forth life. The whole world being attracted by the passion of Your love.

What a strange God You are, as I have said so often before. Your love demands response, whether it be from the trees and the flowers or from the swirling galaxies which, unlike my tree (actually John Daley's tree), are not alive for all their fire. And above all from Your creatures which share in Your capacity for knowledge and love. You want us to respond to You. Unlike the tree we have a choice. I am sorry for all the times I have been unresponsive. Help me to burst into flame in response to Your love as the tree has over this weekend.

Help me to love You more.

May 23, 1996 — Chicago

My Love,

I went to breakfast with Dick Phelan this morning. I continue to impressed by the combination of idealism and heritage Catholicism in his life. He is a good man. Take care of him.

I think my condition improves. I am now able to get up in the morning with only the usual difficulties.

I was dead tired when I stopped working last night at ten o'clock — against all my rules!

I love You. Help me to love You more.

May 26, 1996 — Grand Beach

My Love,

Today during the Memorial day weekend I want to reflect on some of the dead — Leo Suenens, Dan Cantwell, and the young single mother of two (age twenty) who died on her first night of work on an expressway construction gang, killed by a hit-and-run driver. Three very different people, all tragic losses. In each case, Dan's less than the other two perhaps, losses of great hope and potential. Cardinal Suenens was the great hope of the Church thirty years ago during the Council. His "disgrace" (and his subsequent turn to the Charismatics) is as good a symbol as one can imagine of the deterioration of our hopes after the end of the Council.

Be good to all of them, I beg You, and to all the departed. I mourn for them and for the loss they represent. I mourn too for all humankind, since all things eventually end tragically. The grave eventually swallows us all up with our hopes and our plans and our dreams. Life ends bitterly.

There is no escape from that truth, though we may try to pretend that there is. Indeed we have to pretend that there is if we are to keep on working and dreaming. All dreams come true and no dreams come true and that is the lesson of human life.

I am throwing myself this coming week into my biggest enterprise ever, doing my share to foster a climate for the next papal election in which democracy and pluralism are the vital issues. Both the study and the book are intended to raise that question in the United States and around the world. I believe that this is the proper time, indeed the perfect time, to do it. Again I see Your wisdom in postponing the publication of the book till now.

I expect disappointment. I have bitten off a lot, more than makes any sense. But that doesn't mean that I will work any less hard for the book.

Help me. Help the project. I beg You.

And I love You.

May 27, 1996 — Grand Beach

My Love,

Two passages about drinking I read today — "When you are intoxicated with divine love, you see God in all things" (Ramakrishna) and "Deep in the wine vault of my love I drank, and when I came out on this open meadow I knew no thing at all."

One says that when we are drunk on Your love, we see You everywhere, and the other says that we see nothing at all. Which of course in the rhetoric used to mean the same thing.

I am not drunk that way. How long has it been since I've had a chance to engage in contemplation! Those interludes were the closest I've come to divine intoxication, and I have almost given them up. Not because I did not enjoy them, but because the world closes in on all sides.

I will try today, I say here. I hope I mean it. Please help me.

I love You.

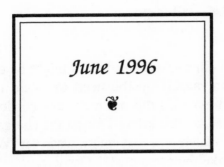

June 1, 1996 — Chicago

My Love,

I feel very fragile this morning, discouraged, beaten, pushed to the end of my rope. I don't think that the Pope study is having the impact it should have. I doubt that my novel *White Smoke* will be a success. All the time and effort and money I put in this project is wasted. And this physically draining promotion tour on which I am going is also a waste. All the hard work of my life is a waste. Life is tragic loss, and if we knew that at the beginning we wouldn't try so hard and we'd enjoy our few years more.

Do I believe all of that? Well, just now I do. But I haven't lived that way and won't live that way for however many or few years You give me.

I am, however, really down, unaccountably down. Or maybe not so unaccountably.

Too many things happen at the same time. I guess that's it. Too much hatred and envy and resentment. I wish I could go back to bed and sleep all day to avoid it.

Anyway, I love You. Protect me on this trip.

June 8, 1996 — Chicago

My Love,

Back in Chicago, exhausted as might be expected and feeling run ragged by the need to catch up with both s-mail and e-mail. I did not make any entries during the trip because, as You know, I forgot the charger for my toy computer, which was real smart, wasn't it? With any luck I won't make the same mistake tomorrow.

I have not lost my patience and have indeed remained charming throughout the trip. Right now I feel that I can make no guarantees about the West Coast. However, I promise to try. Protect me and take care of me.

I love You. Help me to continue to work for You and for Your love.

June 19, 1996 — Chicago

My Love,

I'm afraid that I have not been here in meditations for four days and in my contemplative mood even less. I'm so sorry, really I am. You know the excuses that I would make, the tour, twenty-four-hour flu, total exhaustion and depression. It's over now except for a few phone calls — and maybe one more trip to N.Y. and Los Angeles. I thank You for taking care of me on the trip. I thank You even more for Grand Beach, where I will go this afternoon after the Loyola reception is over and begin to rest. I thank You for all the blessings and for keeping my patience and my Irish glibness, which has enabled me to field all the questions, though it wears a little thin on occasion. Help me to settle in now and do nothing for a while.

I love You. Help me to love You more.

June 22, 1996 — Grand Beach

My Love,

At last at Grand Beach and a beautiful day too, one of the rare ones this spring and now summer. It is to be enjoyed. I also, however, have two wedding anniversaries to do. And, as always, the windows are torture to open.

But no complaints. It's summer, my season above all others, and I propose to relax and enjoy it. And return to serious prayer, which I have neglected for so long, partly because of the tour and partly because of my anemia, which is now, three months after the incident, cured. For which many, many thanks.

Life doesn't mean much without prayer. And I haven't prayed much lately. Today is the day that summer begins for both my body and soul.

I love You. I thank You for this time of renewal.

June 23, 1996 — Grand Beach

My Love,

Another nice day, for which thanks, and another interlude of contemplation, for which, no matter how imperfect it was, even more thanks. Tomorrow I must go in to see the doctor and then on Thursday the dentist. Then I'm essentially free unless another national TV appearance comes along.

Wonderful!

I will relax, that I promise You.

And I will go to the beach every day unless driven off by flies.

Time slips through our fingers so rapidly.

I love You.

June 24, 1996 — Grand Beach

My Love,

All went well at the doctor's today, for which many, many thanks. *White Smoke* is selling out all around the country, which is also very good news indeed and for which I am very grateful.

I love You. Help me to love You more.

June 25, 1996 — Grand Beach

My Love,

When I thought I might be dying last March, I was ready to go, ready to give up all the struggle, ready to find peace of whatever kind. The peace I felt then, however temporarily, was a peace of trust.

I do trust despite all the mysteries and puzzles, all the suffering and cruelty, all the agony and frustration, all the broken dreams, and all the hatred and envy. I don't trust enough and I should trust more. I should believe that indeed You do speak to me with the voice of a Mother and that in the final analysis I have been embraced with a Mother's love.

I do believe it, but not strongly enough. Help me to strengthen my belief this day.

I love You.

June 26, 1996 — Grand Beach

My Love,

"Protect me, O Lord, for I go into the forest" — thus a prayer which I read this morning. A simple prayer, a prayer of fear and trust, a thoroughly human prayer, a prayer which I don't say enough.

The ape with her firstborn about which I read in this morning's paper so fiercely protects her child. How much more fiercely do You protect us who are Your children.

Help me, as I go into the forest of my life today, to cling to Your love.

I love You.

June 27, 1996 — Grand Beach

My Love,

I received an e-mail this morning from a woman who lamented all the good men who are priests who would be such better men if they had a woman in their lives. I'm not sure that marriage makes anyone better, save in that it forces some of the rough edges into a state of polish. If you are not a good and thoughtful man before marriage, marriage won't turn you into a good and thoughtful man. Some priests are selfish boors; so are many married men. Just sleeping in the same bed with a woman does not transform the personality.

Unless we are in Your embrace from the beginning and tenderized by it, then we don't become human.

Help me to appreciate that embrace each day.

I love You.

June 28, 1996 — Grand Beach

My Love,

In the readings today, You are presented again as Lady Wisdom, one of Your most attractive and appealing masks, metaphors, images, sacraments — call it what we may. I know lots of lady wisdoms, women who are charming, demanding, smart, and tender. Lady Wisdom is simply that kind of woman writ large. She runs the universe and the world and everything else besides just as my wise women run the lives of those for whom they care.

Sometimes, in my observation, the human ladies wisdom try to run too much and become oppressive. They want to protect from harm so they try to make their charges' decisions for them. You are not that way. You let us run our own lives, more or less, but take care of us just the same.

Right now I feel the need of Your maternal care as I struggle through the final years of my life with a certain sense of discouragement over my many failures and my mistakes and disappointments. The man who attacked me in the *Seattle Times* said that my life was a tragic failure because the Vatican did not take me seriously. Ha! I don't consider my life a failure, especially not for that reason. But I have missed opportunities and bungled others. More seriously, I have worked too much, which is a very great failure indeed. And I have let the envious get to me, which is also a great failure.

But You still love me and care for me. No matter what happens You will always love me and will eventually wipe away all my tears. Help me to rest secure and serene in the envelope of Your love.

I love You.

June 29, 1996 — Grand Beach

My Love,

In one of my readings today, someone prays that You might keep him from trying to do too much and from trying to do it all at once. That prayer hit me hard because it describes me perfectly — someone who is trying to do everything at once and to do it all at the same time.

I have spread myself thin throughout my life as a priest. Thus as June comes to an end I find myself with five articles to write, counting a column, a book review, my homilies for July, a chapter in a chain novel, and my Irish paper for Oxford. That's a lot. I'm not sure which one of those I should have turned down. But it is too much, isn't it?

Each of them isn't much, but the combination of all of them is kind of overwhelming, especially since I am trying to wind down toward a real vacation during July.

Some things I do because it's easier to do them than to say no.

But that is a philosophy that I ought not to pursue. Still, as I look over the list I realize that it is only the chain novel that I could have honestly passed up.

Still one must do what one can.

I was able to waterski yesterday. I was able to get up, which is no small feat at sixty-eight. I didn't ski well, but then I never did, did I?

No new projects when I get all these things wrapped up, that I promise.

I love You.

July 2, 1996 — Grand Beach

My Love,

My reading this morning emphasizes Your maternal aspect, Your fertility in presiding over life, all kinds of life from the mosquitoes who have flourished in the wet weather this spring, to the giant trees. Just now in early July everything seems to flourish, especially trees and bushes which have grown tremendously here since last summer, so that I'm losing my view of the lake again. In my garden the flowers have erupted because of the sun last week. Yellows and reds and purples against the thick green. How wonderful, how marvelous, how spectacular an evidence of You! Life and life superabundant, that's the Midwest in early July. I must believe in life, no matter what other and contrary data are revealed. There cannot be life if there is not a lifegiver.

However, and with all due respect to fertility as a metaphor, the metaphor of women which appeals to me the most as a sacrament of You is their mystery and their charm. The attraction that women hold for men (and vice versa, naturally) is a faint hint of Your attraction. When I find a woman attractive I am receiving a

message from You.... How stupid spiritual writers, theologians, and church leaders in ages past were to find this
attraction evil.

For humans perhaps the best metaphor of all for You
is the opposite gender. It is so unfortunate that we don't
preach that enough and insist on it always. But Christian-
ity is still in its early phases.

July 3, 1996 — Grand Beach

My Love,

Good news on the book front: *White Smoke* has made
the Ingram bestseller list, currently as number 14 and
apparently rising.

Thank You for the good news. Thank You for the good
weather. Thank You for the relaxation which is slowly taking over my body and soul. A way to go yet, but at least I
am going in the right direction.

I love You. Protect all during the holiday tomorrow.

July 9, 1996 — Grand Beach

My Love,

I believe that You are a Mother more than anything
else, that the maternal metaphor is the best of them all,
that You love me as a mother loves her newborn child. If
only I could throw myself on that love and stop worrying
about everything, knowing that no matter what happens I
remain serene on Your breast. It is not easy of course, but I
don't even come close to it. I need help to realize that I am
embraced by infinite mother love. But at least I know it to
be true, and that is a first step.

Love is everywhere. And wherever it is, it reveals You. As I said in a note to Sebastian Moore the other day, the fact that we can love is a proof that there is love, which is to say Love. What a complex and baffling thing it is. But how overwhelmingly attractive.

On Sunday I was reading on the beach. A couple walked by, late thirties perhaps, good condition. As they passed me the man very tentatively put his arm around the woman, as if he expected that he would be rebuffed. After a moment she put her arm around him and sort of snuggled against him. Because of their swim suits, they both were in contact with each other's bare flesh. She patted his back lightly. It was a natural, almost routine gesture, that perhaps no one else on the beach, except You and I, noted. A reconciliation after a spat? A preliminary to love making? A recommitment to their union?

And how much else besides?

You were there with them, of that I'm certain. You reveled in their gesture of affection. You smiled complacently to Yourself. Because You had them. They would not escape from one another, not that day anyway and hence not from You. For You it was a great day on the beach.

Nothing elaborate, nothing very subtle. Merely a common, ordinary, mild exchange of affection as part of an ongoing affectionate relationship. Yet the impact was surely magical, to say nothing of gracious.

All very clever on Your part. I bet You even laugh. Two of Your children whom You had designed for one another falling victim once again to Your schemes.

Either that is true — and I know it is — or life is devoid of meaning.

I love You.

July 10, 1996 — Grand Beach

My Love,

There is a charming image in one of my readings this morning — from a German Hassidic Jew. If You had cattle, he says, and You asked him to watch them for You, he would not charge You — though he charges everyone else whose cattle he watches!

Quaint, simple, and without much theological depth? Sure, but that doesn't matter because finally faith is quaint, simple, and without much theological depth. The steps before the second naiveté may be complex, critical, and steeped in theological reasoning. But the second, like the first, is a simple leap of faith: "Now I believe, help my unbelief!"

So often I insist that You are a person, an affectionate vulnerable person, because that's the way Your self-disclosure presents Yourself. But I tend to live as though You are not a Thou but rather an It and don't really need my attention, my care, and my love.

It is very hard to picture You as depending on me the way so many humans depend on me, the way even that a human parent depends on her child. Yet that is the image I should carry in my head throughout the day, not how much must be done in the course of the day.

You are as lovely and as fragile as the flower in my perennial garden, as the regenerating beach, as the ladybug, as the grass, as a human lover. Help me to always increase my faith in You and Your need for me, even though rationally I must wonder how the One who caused the Big Bang could possibly need me.

But You do. You have said so, and I must try to live that way as the summer days quickly fly off on me.

I love You. Help me to love You more.

July 13, 1996 — Grand Beach

My Love,

The reading this morning says that You know me as I am. That's for sure. There is no point in pretending with You or trying to hide or claiming virtue that I do not have. You know my secret thoughts and desires, my angers and my sensitivities, my needs and my worries. Many of the things You know about me, most of them probably, are things I would not want others to know and of which I am ashamed myself. I am utterly open and transparent to You.

Yet, just the same, You love me. Why I do not know, but that is the way it is with love, isn't it? I do not deserve to be loved. I have never merited love. But nonetheless I am loved, and for that I am extremely grateful. Help me to love You more.

July 14, 1996 — Grand Beach

My Love,

Many of my readings this month have to do with light. I should understand such readings because light is so important to my life. Light or the absence thereof has a tremendous impact on me. These last two weeks of sunny weather have lifted my spirits. A couple of days of clouds and rain and I find myself gloomy and discouraged — even though none of the objective realities in my life change at all.

However, the writers mean something different than sunlight, something deeper, richer, more important and more powerful.

They mean, of course, Your light, which enables them to see in the deepest darkness, the darkness of suffering

and pain and discouragement and failure and death —
and the worst darkness of all, the darkness in which You
are mysteriously both present and absent.

I know neither that darkness nor that light, though
occasionally in my fitful and distracted contemplative interludes I see a kind of light, a white light which enables
me to experience joy and peace and happiness, feelings
which linger only partially during the day.

I must try to find ways to recall that light in the course
of the day, to be more aware of it, to permit You to bathe
me more in it.

I do not know how this light relates to the light of
which the authors speak, but I know what it is: it is the
light of Your love breaking into my hectic hurried life.
Help me to be more open to that light and that love so that
I can say with greater feeling and depth that I love You.

July 20, 1996 — Grand Beach

My Love,

A glorious summer day, for which many thanks. Kids,
beach, pool, guests — and I'm happy with them all.
Slowly, slowly the summer rest is sinking in. For which
much gratitude.

I love You.

July 21, 1996 — Grand Beach

My Love,

I have been reflecting on the terrible airplane tragedy
over Long Island, the sad, angry relatives on TV, and the
high school French club which was wiped out.

Life is tragic. We all die. It is especially tragic when young people die because of fanatics. There are calls to make airline travel safer, which I can only applaud, but I wonder why there are not louder calls to make life safer by controlling nicotine and guns and ending the reign of street gangs in the nation's cities. Airline disasters are more dramatic I guess.

I believe that You will wipe away every tear, including my own. I know You will, but sometimes it is hard to believe that strongly enough. Help my unbelief.

I love You.

July 22, 1996 — Grand Beach

My Love,

Do I believe in life after death? If I do, why am I offended to hear people proclaim that belief on television after a disaster? Why was I particularly offended by a churchman's oily words on TV?

I guess the reason is that I think the issue is a lot more complicated than they make it sound. They seem to short-circuit the ugly, destructive tragedy of death. The grief, the pain, the terror, the long road to recovery. And also the mystery. I don't mind it from the families of the victims, because they're talking in Catholic code and reasserting their belief that love is as strong as death — that death can never win out over love.

But that church leader sounded empty and bland.

A priest, it seems to me, needs to acknowledge fully the terror of death before he reasserts hope. I'm sure that this resonates better with people because it is the way they feel.

I love You. Strengthen my faith.

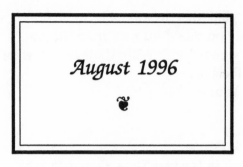

August 1996

August 8, 1996 — Grand Beach

My Love,

There's a major to-do now about life on Mars because scientists have found evidence of water and microbes on a meteorite from Mars. I guess I'm not so excited about it because I take it for granted that someone like You, as exuberant and as enthusiastic as You are, would create rational life just everywhere.

The media paradigms are trotted out for such events. What does this do to religion and to our notion that we are special?

What nonsense! Some fundamentalists may think that religion is affected. Surely we don't. Moreover, all rational life is special because it is made in Your image and likeness, however faint.

Whence comes this notion that You are constrained and rigid, that You are limited in what You can do by our dogmas and our fears? Maybe because so many of our church leaders are themselves so constrained by fear.

Anyway, I'm glad we've begun to catch up with Your splendor as it manifested itself so tentatively on Mars.

115

I'm also glad that it was able to manifest itself more definitively on this third rock from the sun.

And I wonder with Wilfred Meynel in what shape You trod the Pleiades.

I love You.

August 15, 1996 —
Mary's Day in Harvest Time, Grand Beach

My Love,

Mary represents Your maternal love. I've received a few notes recently on e-mail complaining about my reference to You as womanly. Nasty notes, warning me of modernism and the danger I represent to faith. A mix of ignorance and self-righteousness. I resist the temptation to strike back and ignore them instead. They're not interested in the richness of the tradition but only their narrow little obsessions.

One of the readings this morning distinguishes between the "hidden child" and the "secret friend," aspects of the personality which are in conflict. The hidden child wants to strike out; the secret friend wants to laugh.

Help me listen to the secret friend in the present time of trial.

I love You.

August 17, 1996 — Grand Beach

My Love,

Back from New York to a busy day yesterday and today. Dead tired. I have ninety thousand words done on *Irish Whisky* and may well finish it tomorrow. As always at the end of a book, I worry that it doesn't work. I'll have to see when I begin to revise it.

The sociology meeting was good, not enough time, but I'm glad I spent only a day there.

I really am discouraged, worse than ever I think. I have to pull out of it.

It's astonishing that I can still work regularly and routinely when I feel so disheartened. Maybe that's healthy or maybe not.

I think I don't respect myself enough.

I've tried several times to do my contemplation at the beach, but there's too much noise down there. Maybe when I get up in the morning I should go outside and try to pray. I'll see tomorrow.

I love You.

August 28, 1996 — Grand Beach

My Love,

John Horgan's book on science continues to fascinate me. It is clear that the cosmos is an exceedingly complicated place. Also an exuberant place, full of wonder, though Horgan doesn't say that.

There is not enough wonder or surprise or awe in my life. Quite the contrary, there is almost none of those marvelous qualities. I drag along, discouraged, depressed, sometimes even bitter. I should be ashamed of myself.

The end of summer, as You know, always gets to me, especially when, as in every summer, I feel I've wasted summer over the trivial things.

So little wonder or surprise about the splendor of this place, this time, this summer? The answer is that I want to cling to summer as a way of clinging to life. Instead of enjoying its splendor and surprise in their revelatory transience, I try to cling to it so that it won't be lost.

Is that what's going on? Well, something like that. Not good.

I'm sorry. I love You.

August 31, 1996 — Grand Beach

My Love,

I'm devastated. The Cardinal's cancer has returned. The doctors tell him he has less than a year to live. A terrible blow to the Church and the Archdiocese and to me. The last of the great churchmen of the post-conciliar era. You know what You're doing and as always I accept Your will. Still it is very hard. Help him. Help us all.

And if You have an unused miracle around, now would be a good time to use it.

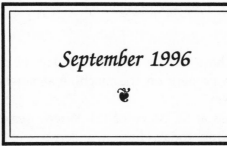

September 1, 1996 — Grand Beach

My Love,

How wonderful the Cardinal was on television yesterday, and in his phone calls to me: a man of faith, never more fully a priest. Applause from the media and a choked thank you from Mary Anne in the name of everyone. Death is not an enemy but a friend. I believe that for sure.

I've been through this twice, first Cardinal Meyer and now Joe. And as usual Chicago is at the mercy of others who do not care a fig about the clergy and laity of the Archdiocese. Grim days ahead. Something has to be done to protect a city, people, and priests from the terrible system of choosing bishops.

Life is ultimately tragic, isn't it? Comedy is more ultimate but that comes later.

A Jesuit friend called last night. Why is God mad at the Church? he asked. There are plenty of good reasons why You should be angry at us, we have so twisted Your message that it is unrecognizable.

I will cope with the loss of Joe, but a little bit goes out of life. I love You.

September 22, 1996 — Chicago

My Love,

I seem to have lost the last twenty days of reflections. They have to be here on the machine somewhere, but I can't find them.

I said Mass at St. Mary of the Woods yesterday and Christ the King today. Both wonderful experiences. I thank You for the grace of the liturgy.

Joe goes to Rome tomorrow to plead for Chicago. Not much hope as far as I can see. But help him please.

I love You.

September 27, 1996 — Chicago

My Love,

Some enjoyable days coming up — Degas, Symphony, Emerald Ball, Opera, Bears, and another opera. Then off to Germany. Too much culture for a weekend? I suspect so with all the other stuff. Help me to enjoy it and see Your beauty in it, Your endlessly mysterious, baffling, puzzle-creating beauty.

Which I love. Help me to love it more.

September 28, 1996 — Chicago

My Love,

Wonderful day yesterday. Good times. So much of Your beauty reflected in Degas and Brahms. Thank You for everything.

Must have been a score of people who came up to me at the grand Emerald Ball and congratulated me about the things I'd been saying on TV about possible successors to the Cardinal. Too bad Rome does not understand the intensity of feelings on the subject in Chicago.

I'm going to write today about why I am "still" a Catholic for the book Marilyn and Kevin Ryan are editing. That should give me much to reflect on.

However, You know what I'm going to do now?

I'm going back to bed. I'm dead tired.

I love You.

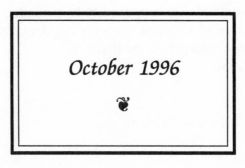

October 1996

October 1, 1996 — Chicago

My Love,

Off to Cologne in a few hours. Take care of me and protect me and keep me patient and gentle during the trip.

A lot of thoughts about death because of the film *Spitfire Grill*, the explosion at a propane factory in Indiana, and my memory of an accident on the Dan Ryan Expressway when it opened, so many years ago.

A twenty-three-year-old man, new on the job, tried to stop his truck from entering the express lane in which trucks are forbidden. He tipped over and died in the crash.

How horrible, I thought then, and still remember it every time I come to 71st street. Poor kid, a new job, a new life, all wiped out by a single error in judgment. He's probably forgotten now, most of the time even by those who loved him.

Except, I have to believe, by You. But what is the world to come like. What is he doing now? I know we can't fathom it. But still the question persists.

I'm sure You wiped every tear from his eye when You received him in Your arms. But still I'm baffled.

I understand: I'm supposed to be baffled.

Take care of all those who die accidentally and especially those who grieve for them.

I love You.

October 2, 1996 — Cologne

My Love,

I'm back in one of my favorite places in all the world! The ride up along the Rhine from Frankfurt was lovely. The Holiday Inn is very nice indeed. Alas I came down with a bad case of motion sickness on the train. Awful. I feel better now.

So much history along the Rhine, so much suffering, so much blood. Thank God that the wars which have split this part of the world since the Thirty Years War seem now to be over. Help me to stay close to You while I'm here.

I love You.

October 5, 1996 — Cologne

My Love,

We're on to some interesting research here about You. Or rather about Your triumph over secularization and atheism. The "real" atheists in our sample, those who reject both You and the probability of life after death, are about 10 percent of our sample. But if one looks only at the countries which were never socialist (or in the case of Poland, never really socialist) the average drops to about 7 percent. Then one looks at the socialist countries and finds 11 percent in Hungary, 13 percent in Russia, 12 percent in

Slovenia. Thus for all its militant atheism, socialism increased only marginally the proportion of atheists in the world. The exception is East Germany, where the rate is 40 percent, an astonishing proportion. Socialism worked only where there was a past of Nazi oppression of religion and Teutonic efficiency. It will be interesting to see what happens there.

But You are alive and well and living in Europe!

That will be a neat finding to publish. I hope You give me points for it!

This morning I love You powerfully. I feel that love, and I thank You.

October 6, 1996 — Cologne

My Love,

I spent most of the day working on our article about You and those who reject You completely — the hard-core atheists. I find that most of them made the decision very early in life, when they were still children. Astonishing. They never had a chance to reflect on You as adults. In great part they were either victims of intense manipulation in the socialist countries or, I suspect, of disrupted families in their childhood. Poor people. It makes me feel blessed once again.

Thank You.

I know You love the hard-core atheists as much as You love me and that You will take care of them.

Help me to love You more and to do whatever I can for them.

October 12, 1996 — Cologne

My Love,

Last day here. Off very early tomorrow morning before my transcontinental weekend — from Chicago to Santa Barbara to New York and back to Chicago in five days. Not a good idea.

I look out the window and I see the Apostle Church, the busy Rudolfplatz, the shopping streets, and in the distance the elegant twin towers of the Dom. Two thousand years of history in a modern context. On CNN as I type this there is a terrifying story of a ride down the Congo in the decaying country of Zaire. Horrible.

How does it all fit together? What about all the people who have suffered and died here and in Zaire? Why? I don't know. I'll never figure it out. My own chronic (what should I call it?) discouragement is worse as the weariness from the trip closes in on me.

I think about the Church as the Dom and the other churches impinge on my imagination — superstitious, profligate, corrupt, yet faithful in its own way. Are we any better than they were? Certainly no less corrupt or insensitive than they were. Maybe more hypocritical?

Why did You decide that Your followers should be human beings? Angels could have done a much better job.

I guess I'm on overload. Anyway I love You. It's been a good trip. Take care of me on the way home.

October 14, 1996 — Chicago

My Love,

Back in Chicago and catching up, the usual mad, tense time while I fight off all the silly mail (which I answer nonetheless) and do all the silly work, and maybe accomplish a little bit of something.

And St. Teresa tells me this morning that You are everything, which I believe and I read that I have a secret wine cellar and a buried treasure in my soul, which I also believe but for which, alas, I have so little time.

My computer still isn't fixed. It has been a good purgatory experience for me, eight months of frustration!

I'm going to have to try to contemplate this afternoon. I hope I get everything cleared away by then.

I love You. Help me to love You more. And more confidently.

October 17, 1996 — Chicago

My Love,

I saw the Cardinal yesterday. His time is down to a couple of months. Rome will not give him a coadjutor. Chicago is in deep trouble.

The *New York Times* interview I did with him was, I think, a good one. I was so sad that I could hardly do it. What a wonderful, brave man he is, what a fine witness to the Church, what a great example to all of us.

How tragic it all is.

How foolish are all the other things in life when one faces death.

How exemplary he is.

Our worries simply don't matter. They don't do any good.

Help me to approach death with the same grace.

I love You.

October 20, 1996 — En route to JFK

My Love,

Shea says I should view the ride from Santa Barbara to New York this Sunday just like a ride downtown on the 95th Street Bus. Not a bad idea, but this bus is bumpy and hot, even in business class, to which I was just barely able to upgrade with my miles.

Till now I've been all right on this trip, but the bumps get to my inner ear and I'm deteriorating. Only one more night away from home after tonight. But Santa Barbara is a beautiful city.

Someone I was talking to yesterday said that he no longer accepted the theory that You were love. Rather he said, You are a black cloud that doesn't care much about us, certainly not about what we were eating for supper last night.

He's a Catholic, but it seems to me that he rejects the heritage, not only Jesus and St. John, but also Isaiah and some of the other prophets. It's kind of like my other friend's notion that You are a cosmic buzz. Or Ingmar Bergman's spider.

Dark mysticism indeed!

Jesus came, I believe, to tell us that it is not that way. So I think what he said was a rejection of Jesus too. He cited science as a grounds for such a belief, though not all scientists conclude that.

I admit that sometimes the data are confusing and that one can make a case for the black cloud, but there are also other data, are there not?

Faith is a leap into the dark, into the fog of mystery as I said in my paper yesterday. I've made a leap of trust in favor of You. I don't think I'll regret it.

So You are not a dark cloud, even if You are fog. The

fog is not darkness but blinding light. It is You. You are Mystery and when I jump into the fog, I jump into You.

I love You.

October 21, 1996 — Rhinebeck, N.Y.

My Love,

The talks here went well today, three of them. I am tired and eager to go home but not completely wiped out yet.

Terrible rain, but lovely countryside.

Thank You for the graces of the trip.

Home soon — great sacrament!

I love You.

October 22, 1996 — Going home from Newburgh, N.Y.

My Love,

Very bumpy ride home.

I'm grateful for the blessings of this trip — and for having survived without making too many mistakes. It will be so wonderful to get home.

A lot of talk about religion and about You. I am more than every dismayed by theology's propensity to stand between You and the people You love. Both in the discussions last night and in the book I've been reading — *Maps of Heaven and Hell* — I hear the arrogance of theology which draws lines and boundaries and sits in judgment on people and their lives and loves, their fears and their horrors, their hopes and their failures. In a way it is worse than the man in California who wanted to reduce You to a black cloud who pays little attention to us.

For that did Jesus come into the world?

This opposition between Torah and Jesus which preoccupied us last night offends me. I don't know why we have to fight over it. Folly, folly folly!

Both are revelations of You. Should not that be enough? Theology has to reflect, define, and be precise. Yet does that mean it has to separate? I don't think so.

Religions are different perhaps irrevocably, yet they have much in common, certainly all religions of the Book do. I am more than ever convinced that we should listen to one another before we argue.

But much of the argument gets in Your way, I think.

And I love You.

October 28, 1996 — Chicago

My Love,

You are hiding everywhere on this lovely day. Help me to stay in touch with You as I work through the day. Help me to enjoy the opera tonight. Help me to relax. Help me to be aware of Your presence. Help me to be cheerful. Help me to put aside my angers and frustrations. Help me to love.

I do love You.

I will die sometime soon. I don't know when. It might be ten years; it might be a couple of months. I don't know of what or how. But I do know I will die. If I were to die today, I would feel perhaps some relief as the time drew near because the struggle would be over, and some disappointment because the struggle would not have been won.

But why the struggle? Why cannot I dismiss all the conflicts and battles, all the lost causes? They make no difference. You love me and so do countless humans. Is that not enough? Why is there so much conflict in my soul?

Help me to get rid of it and to approach the end with the serenity that You want me to have.

Help me.

Again I say that I love You.

October 29, 1996 — Chicago

My Love,

We saw Menotti's *The Consul* last night, as chilling an "opera" as one could imagine. It made me reflect even more on my recent trip to what used to be East Germany. What evil regimes they were and how fortunate the world is to have less of them than it once did. The totalitarian temptation is always there, however, is it not?

Even, as much as I hate to say it, in the Church. I fail to see much difference between many of our leaders and the Socialist bureaucrats. Both serve an ideology without thought or conscience in the name of sacred goals but in fact to protect their own power. Terrible people.

One can and indeed must be loyal to the Catholic tradition without sanctifying those power-hungry bureaucrats. It's not easy because they pretend to have a monopoly on You.

I intend to remain inside and to continue to fight against them, regardless. I must not, however, permit myself to grow angry at those who agree with me but attack me for saying what they are afraid to say.

Help the Church, even if it often doesn't deserve or even want Your help.

I love You.

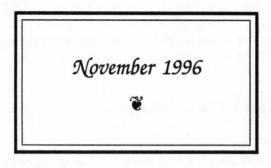

November 3, 1996 — Chicago

My Love,

I read the Bernstein-Politi book [*The Mind of John Paul II: Origin of His Thought and Action*, Doubleday, 1996] about the Pope yesterday for a review in the *Chicago Tribune.* It was a profoundly disturbing book not so much because of the allegations about the CIA spying on priests in Central America and relaying that information to the Vatican, as for some of the stories about the Pope, toward whom the authors are clearly sympathetic. When one clears away all the Pope worship in which many Catholics engage, he does not appear to be a nice man. Nor do the people he appoints as bishops. I worry about the Church with such people in charge. How can they so badly misread the signs of the times? How can they be so out of touch with the life of ordinary people?

The book is profoundly disillusioning. Not merely that the leadership of the Church is so human; for that I am long since prepared. But that it is so stupid.

I guess one should never put one's hope in institutions, not even the Church. One's hope should rest only in You.

Yet I am dismayed by the opportunities lost.

Well, one must keep the faith and keep trying, though
the walls of opposition are so strong. I love You.

November 5, 1996 — Chicago

My Love,

Election day. I voted promptly at six o'clock because
it will be a busy day. Looks like Clinton and a Repub-
lican congress. Same old thing. More gridlock. People
are dumb.

I watched some of John Shea's video tapes last night.
Good stuff. In particular the story of Cro-Magnon man,
the teen disappointed by not getting a full box of popcorn. It was only half full, so the young woman behind
the counter filled it to overflowing. Like You do.

How much I have been given! Overwhelming gifts.
They don't make me particularly happy, I'm afraid, and
in great part because I want more. Also I want the gift
without the price that has to be paid. How foolish of me.
I should be more than satisfied. And I should realize that
the price comes with the territory. I am marginal because
I do marginal things. Too bad for those who make me
marginal, but not worth ruining my peace and joy.

I accept the bad with the good and rejoice in all the
good You have given me and thank You for it. Help me
to sustain this attitude in whatever years of life remain.

I love You.

November 7, 1996 — Chicago

My Love,

Jack Shea's story this morning is the wonderful story
about the monk who rode in on an ox and told the towns-

people that he was looking for an ox. They all laughed at him. He went to the next town with the same plea. They laughed again. Finally someone said to him, "You're riding on an ox; why are you looking for one?" To which the monk, very clever man, replied that his search for an ox when he was riding on one was no more foolish than their search for God who is already within them.

The point, my Love, is well taken. All through our lives we're searching for You, and You are actually lurking inside us, ready, willing and eager. I believe that firmly, yet my attempts at contemplation this morning were terribly unsuccessful because I am so tired. Maybe Dr. Phee is right about conserving my energy.

Or maybe I should have stayed in bed for an extra hour.

Anyway, despite my weariness I shall try again today to be aware of Your presence, even closer to me than the ox to the monk who was riding on him.

I love You.

November 10, 1996 — Chicago

My Love,

I said Mass at another parish last night. The book signing afterward was a mess, not enough books and the wrong books too.

However the people were very nice. I was struck by faith — a son just released from prison, a lesbian daughter, and somehow pride in both of them. The pastor, incredibly overworked, but still hopeful. It was a good experience. There is so much more to the Church than the idiots who run it.

Also I received a letter yesterday from a very angry woman whose mother had just died after much suffering.

She was mad at You and mad at me because she figures I'm somehow responsible for You. You did not answer her prayers, she said.

A lot of people who are angry at death become angry at You. Pointless, I guess, but You're a good inkblot. You claim to be a lover, they say, but You really don't act like one.

No explanation is good for that problem. One tries. I know You are a lover and that like all lovers and all mothers, You will wipe away all the tears and that we will all be young again and all laugh again. And that all will be well and that all manner of things will be well.

But that's in the long run.

Yet there were those two mothers proud of their children. You are certainly present in that love.

And it is that which I love most about You — Your refusal to be limited by anything, especially Church rules.

And the Cardinal is in bed now, poor, poor man. Help him please. And help all of us.

November 14, 1996 — Chicago

My Love,

The Cardinal died, as You well know, at 1:30 this morning, apparently very peacefully. He had finished only yesterday (less than twenty-four hours before he died) the memoir he was dictating.

I'm numb. I knew it was coming of course, yet it is a terrible loss for all of us. I'm happy that he did not linger and suffer. And I'm happy for him, now that he's gone home where we all want to go, though not without fear and hesitation. He has indeed shown us the way to go.

I got home from Atlanta yesterday afternoon just

after the Archdiocese announced that his condition was "grave." Phones rang all afternoon and into the evening. I was a basket case, to put it mildly. Then I was awakened at 3:30, as I had expected to be, to do both *Good Morning America* and Channel 5 local. June Rosner said that I did well. Short of Your approval, what more could I ask for?

I'm still in a half trance, tired, shocked, grief-stricken. Some day I will go too. Joseph taught us how to die. Help me also to be an example of faith.

I love You.

November 16, 1996 — Chicago

My Love,

Saturday, a grim lonely Saturday with the Cardinal gone. Ken Velo called last night. I grieve especially for him and for Sister Brian. He was upbeat as he always is. He told me that Joe suffered considerably toward the end, especially from the back pain which was unrelated to the cancer.

How awful it all is. I keep on with my work, because that's all you can do, but my heart isn't in anything. I worry about the future here. I worry about the Church without him. I worry about the next papal election in his absence. But these worries are exceeded by my sadness. I shall miss him, despite the differences we had. Most of the differences were created by others, bad, miserable people that they were, begrudgers.

Still I lament that I let them keep us at a distance for so long. I'm not proud of myself for the way I behaved. Yet when you are under attack from all sides you tend to see enemies everywhere. What was worse in those days is that they were everywhere, and there were more of them than I would have thought.

Nonetheless I did not act well under the strain, did I? Not at all, not at all.

I wish it could have been otherwise, but it was not. At least I made the most of the opportunities of the past five years, for which I am thankful.

What a wonderful, powerful figure he was in this city! As Kenny said last night, he would have loved the news coverage.

But as I said to him, he knows about it and loves it.

I regret that he never understood what once went wrong between us and who made it go wrong, but I did not want to attack other people.

Terrible melancholy thoughts, I fear. But that's the way this day is.

I love You.

November 17, 1996 — Chicago

My Love,

The grief and mourning continue in this city and the dread of the future. Lots of coverage in the media and a tremendous outpouring of grief and respect, none of which will have any impact on Rome or on the next Archbishop.

There was the first segment of his book in the *Trib* this morning, about how he began to pray. It made me feel sad about the failure of my prayer life. I do devote time to this reflection and I do try to contemplate, but I haven't done it once in this totally crazy week. I am ashamed of myself, but when could I have done it?

The answer, I suppose, is that I could have easily done

it if I wasn't so busy about so many other things. I promise I will devote time to it tonight.

Joe prayed first thing in the morning. Ideally I would swim and then pray first thing every morning, but much of the time that's impossible. I have to work on a way to pray more and better. I need Your help.

I love You.

November 18, 1996 — Grand Beach

My Love,

I go over to Channel 5 in an hour for the broadcast on the procession from the Cardinal's house to the cathedral.

Yucky. Yet it has to be done.

I will try to emphasize the story nature of religion and how the incarnated stories of Catholicism, especially as contained in the rituals, are the principal appeal of the Catholic tradition and how that's the reason why Catholics return.

I'm doing all right, deeply discouraged of course and sad, but life goes on.

I know this will happen to me some day too. Joe was two months younger than I am.

I love You. Please take care of Chicago this time.

November 20, 1996 — Chicago

My Love,

We buried Joe today. Sad, beautiful, wonderful. I'm dead tired. I must get some sleep. I love You.

November 22, 1996 — Chicago

My Love,
   So sad, so sad, so sad. I love You.

November 23, 1996 — Chicago

My Love,
   Still a lot of grief locked up inside me. It will be that way for a while I guess. Hard grief, deep grief, persistent grief. Time is required.
   At some deep level in my personality I can't believe he's gone. He was such a reality in my life that somehow he seems too large to die. I was at the Loyola Med School dinner last night. Ken Velo was there, looked sad and worn, and thanked me for the words on TV about his homily, as I tried to thank him for a wonderful Catholic expression of faith. I felt so sorry for him.
   Well, it's all over now till we all see each other again in a better world. I will miss him. I mourn for him. We will not see his like again.

November 28, 1996 — Thanksgiving, Grand Beach

My Love,
   It's a picture-perfect Thanksgiving Day — clear, sunny, and over here in the snow belt there's a pretty inch of two of the white stuff on the ground. For this sign of cheer and even of hope, I give thanks. Thanks for the fourteen years we had Cardinal Joe with us. Thanks for family and friends.
   Thanks for life and health — and especially my recovery after the St. Patrick's day bleeding.

Thanks for my vocation to the priesthood and for my implacable commitment to it.

Thanks for the stories. Thank You especially for *Blackie at Sea* and *Irish Whisky* and *Star Bright* and *Angel Song*, the novels on which I have worked since last year, and most especially for *Star Bright*.

Thanks for all the good people who like what I write and reassure me of its worth.

Thanks for this house at Grand Beach and for my time in Arizona.

Thanks for good food and good drink and swimming and beaches and waterskiing.

Thanks for the wondrous city of Chicago and for this country.

Thanks for all the other good things with which You have blessed me.

Bless and protect those I love and those I know through the year till next Thanksgiving. Please see that we get a good bishop to replace our departed brother Joseph.

I love You.

November 30, 1996 — Chicago

My Love,

Off to Ireland this afternoon at six. Get there tomorrow morning about eleven. I'm planning on working on my novel all the way across, using the high intensity lamps on the way to Dublin, and then taking an afternoon nap, followed by a melatonin at night. This regime has worked marvels before.

Anyway take care of me on this trip. Help me to be patient, friendly, and relaxed, no matter how grim and depressed I feel.

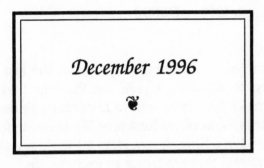

December 1996

December 2, 1996 — Dublin

My Love,

There was a bright light yesterday. Paddy is putting in a new concrete floor to his church in Rathgar so he's been having Mass in the local Presbyterian church! I said Mass there at 7:00 P.M. Both clergy said that if crazy Ian Paisley had found out about it there could have been pickets down here. Still it was the first time I presided over the Eucharist in a Presbyterian church. A small sign of hope.

The Mass was a moving experience. I told my Patricia the Penny Planter story, which they liked, though they didn't smile as much as the American congregations would, doubtless because they are not quite as used to smiling in church as we Yanks are.

They applauded at the end of Mass, however, which was nice.

I'm still basically discouraged, however, profoundly discouraged. Help me.

I love You.

December 3, 1996 — Dublin

My Love,

I stumbled and bumbled around for the last hour or so trying to organize myself for the trip to Kilkenny and Limerick tomorrow and to London on Friday. I'm in good spirits, however, at least now. My presentation is this afternoon. I'm a little sleepy. Help me to do it well.

I'm grateful that I'm living an exciting life.

I love You.

December 5, 1996 — Limerick

My Love,

Yesterday went well enough. In fact, it was grand. Fun people, fascinating time, even an hour nap to catch up with what I lost the night before. And, for which many thanks, a good night's sleep.

I still hate playing the celebrity role. I think I can be charming enough in the circumstances so that I'm a good guest. But I am not a celebrity, not really, and I don't like the game, though it is played with great good will and good intentions and here especially by wonderful and hard-working people who might better forget about me and not waste their time.

Tom Murphy (Archbishop of Seattle) may be dying. Two great Archbishops lost. How terrible. When will the present folly end?

I love You. Keep me together for the rest of the trip. Already I pine for home.

And protect all of those who have been kind to me.

December 7, 1996 — Oxford

My Love,

Paper presentation went fine. Great meeting. Exciting fun. I learned a lot about Ireland and the Irish. I was deeply impressed by the Oxford dons. They are all very, very bright, and also some of them quite arrogant. The Irish scholars are younger and almost as bright but not nearly so self-confident (though funnier). The contrast between the orange and the green is also interesting: the former tend to be more dour, the latter more witty. Like most of the orange folk they are threatened, frightened, difficult, though they pretend to be superior.

I come away with the sense of having had a good meeting and also more pessimistic about the future of Ireland.

One more night and I'm home with a ton of work to do.

Thank You for the excitement. Take care of me on the way home. I love You.

December 8, 1996 — Chicago

My Love,

The data are coming in on our study of what Catholics in the Archdiocese want from their new Archbishop. No consolation for the conservatives, but so what else is new? We will get a conservative anyhow. Why do the research, why spend my own money? Just to get the information out there, I suppose.

I hope to get myself reoriented before the day is over. And next Monday will definitely be a day of recollection. I need it desperately.

I love You. Help me to love You more.

December 13, 1996 — Chicago

My Love,

I'm sure You must get tired of listening to my complaints. I know that You love me and that lovers tolerate and even welcome complaints. I also know that You never get tired. But I'm sorry that I don't break out of my moods more quickly and talk to You more about good things.

Like the day of recollection tomorrow, broken only by the need to go to lunch with someone who needs help. I think the interruption is justified. I am looking forward to the day because I need it so very much.

Today I listen to the hum of the city, the traffic on the avenue, the cry of the ambulance, the shrieks of the fire engines, the hum of traffic — all signs of the vitality and life of the city. And of the fear and the tragedy and despair too.

I know I'll try to write a poem about this tomorrow, a Christmas poem. And I'll post the poems on my web page!

Some of the meals I had recently were not encouraging. I don't mean so much encouraging for me, as encouraging for the human condition. Lots of men and women hurting, some of them people for whom I care. And there's nothing much I can do to ease their pain. Do I know how You feel? A parent to everyone to whom You have given life and nursed and yet powerless to keep them from their paths of self-destruction and agony.

Your job is not easy. Help me to do whatever I can to make it a little easier.

And thank You for the end of the gloom and the end of the jet lag!

I love You.

December 14, 1996 — Chicago

My Love,

A good day of recollection. I am always astonished at how quickly I can regain perspective about myself and my life when I slow down and relax. From that it follows that my madcap exertions can easily be stopped if I only take time off to think about who I am and what I am doing

Why can I not see the positive reinforcement You have showered me with? On a day like this when I put everything back together and understand clearly who I am and what I am doing I understand how much You have surrounded me with Your love. Help me to hang on to that.

Help me to keep alive the re-vision which came so easily today. Grace is everywhere if one is only willing to look at it.

I add the poem which was the turning point this morning.

Christmas Poem

My room is filled with red lights
That recall a Cardinal newly dead
And Christmas presents for the living
Bear the name of a troubled friend

I fall asleep while praying
The bell, always four minutes late,
Snatches me from my peace
I hear the old refrains

You work too hard
(and write too much)
And never had
a thought unpublished

Outside traffic hums
Sirens groan horns scream
Wall-to-wall people
Vanity of vanities

Principled Pelagians
run into the stone wall
of folly, envy, sickness
—human stories gone sour

So many have messed up their lives
And little enough a priest can do
All things end badly
No matter how well begun

All is vanity
Chasing after the wind
Tilting the windmills
Propping up the dike

And yet it is Christmas again
Evergreens and ornaments
Fruits and too much eggnog
Poinsettias and wrapping paper

Not enough sleep,
Far too many people
tempers run amok
Noisy, contentious kids

And light that never fades, never

And never means never. I love You, help me to love
You more.

December 16, 1996 — Chicago

My Love,

We saw the Jazz Nativity last night, which was truly sensational. I had forgotten how powerful it is. The Christmas playlets they did are probably the same sort of thing from which the Christmas narratives we have were put together. I imagined myself back in the mid-first century at a festival celebrating the coming of Jesus before Christmas had been established and before the Gospels were written.

I'm in good spirits as Christmas draws near. Help me to stay that way.

And maybe another day of recollection on Christmas eve.

December 19, 1996 — Chicago

My Love,

Anything I can understand, the poet I read this morning tells me, is not a mystery. So too it is not a wonder or a surprise or a marvel. The comfort lies in fingering the incoherent as true and in suspecting more than the evidence allows.

I love You.

December 20, 1996 — Chicago

My Love,

Life, the poet says this morning, is a chain of failed attempts. That certainly is true. I conclude the day after the press conference about our survey of what kind of bishop Catholics in Chicago want. I conclude that it was ten thousand dollars down the drain. We got some coverage, but not what the story was worth. A few people will read it and a few will remember it.

Nothing ventured, nothing gained. How often have I ventured things and failed, often ignominiously. I believe that's what one must do if one is really a follower of Yours. I'll stand by that faith and take my lumps. So it goes. At least I did something.

Thank You for giving me a chance to take the risk.

I love You.

December 21, 1996 — Chicago

My Love,

The novel is finished!

For which many thanks. I like it and I hope You like it because it is about You and Your love.

It was supposed to be finished a couple of weeks ago but got tied up in a lot of other things. It's kind of a Christmas present to have finished it, both a Christmas present from You to me and, I hope, a Christmas present from me to You.

You are on stage in this one for the whole last chapter. I think my portrait of You will offend some people. I don't much care about them. I hope it will also win some hesitant folk to Your love. I do care much about them. I hope they see in my inadequate portrait of You some hint of who You are. I hope the book flourishes. It probably won't be out till 1999. Will I still be around then?

That is up to You. If You are the God of the story, then I trust You that, whatever, all will be all right.

I love You.

December 23, 1996 — Chicago

My Love,

Two days before Christmas and Chicago is covered in a thick fog. Just this minute lightning and thunder and driving rain. Gale warning on the lake, thirty-five knots, twelve-foot waves. Turn to snow tonight. If it's all the same to You, I'd like to keep the rain. Why do people live in the Midwest?

Tomorrow will be a day of recollection, broken only by breakfast and lunch. More likely a half day of recollection. Help me to do it well. I love You.

December 24, 1996 — Chicago

My Love,

I just finished opening my Christmas cards. What a heart-wrenching experience! So many stories, so many brave, good, generous, faithful, loyal people. So many friends. I would like to keep in touch with all of them, talk to them on the phone once a week. No time of course. As I say, so many friends.

And so much grace! So very much grace! So many grace-full people.

And how inadequate I feel in response to them and their grace. How many people have I let down? How many have I failed? How many expected more from me and didn't get it?

I look back on my life, all the excitement, all the challenge, all the work, all the accomplishment, and I wonder what it means, what it was worth, what it contributes to the story, indeed the romance which started at Bethlehem.

Not much, I fear.

Yet I tried, not always wisely, but at least as hard as I could.

If I believe the novel I'm writing, You love me dearly despite all my failures.

Help me to love You more at this Christmas time.

I love You.

December 25, 1996 — Chicago

My Love,

A bright and sunny Xmas day, albeit the temperature hovers around zero. And snow, many inches of it, tonight. Time for Tucson!

But now I feel reborn, almost jolly, which as You know is not the way I usually am at this time Christmas morning. Help me to keep that attitude through the day.

Today is the day not only of birth but of rebirth, of beginning again, of all things new, of a brand new life. Every day ought to be that way, but that is perhaps too much a strain on our frail organisms. So we have special days like this one when we can all begin again. Help me to live that way at least today.

I love You.

January 1997

January 2, 1997 — Chicago

My Love,

What are You like really? During my much distracted effort at contemplation this morning I experienced You as I almost always do in those interludes as sweet, loving, reassuring, and laughing — a source of joy and hope. That is the way I have portrayed You and related persons in my new novel. Yet that portrait — of a God who laughs and of a mother of Jesus who is mischievous — is not one that is widely accepted and will probably get me in trouble with the hyper-orthodox.

In the book You say that You laugh a lot and weep a lot. This portrait is not at odds with the scripture. But it is certainly at odds with ordinary piety.

Yet if laughter is a human perfection, though less than a perfect perfection, why should it be denied to You?

Why is it necessary that You be presented as solemn and somber and grim and unsmiling? Maybe because religious teachers take themselves so seriously.

I suppose I could ask myself the question why, if I think You are a laughing God, I get so grim and discouraged so often in my life. I experience You as a God of joy and hope and laughter, but I don't live like I believe that experience, much less like I am filled with such an experience. All I can say is that during this new year I will try harder to live that way. Help my unbelief. I love You.

January 3, 1997 — Chicago

My Love,

I'm having a hard time sleeping so I'm up finishing my packing.

Nice event yesterday. President Clinton took *Irish Lace* along for his weekend vacation. He likes what I write, he said, because I write about two of his favorite places — Chicago and Ireland. It was nice for me, even though it's not going to sell many books. You take your compliments where you can find them, right?

Anyway I love You. Help me to love You more. And thanks for the presidential plug.

January 4, 1997 — Chicago

My Love,

Off to Tucson today. I'm glad to go and sad to go, which means that it's the same way as in 1979 when I went for the first time.

Usually I blow the Tucson opportunity for a more relaxed life. Last two years there were two projects, neither one of which worked out. I hope not to do that again.

I thank You for the grace of this change of scenery. Help me to make the most of it. Protect me while I'm gone and protect all those I love. Help me to love You more. Help me to slow down a bit the rush of my life.

I love You.

January 7, 1997 — Tucson

My Love,

Szymborksa in the poems I read this morning is concerned about frailty and survival, this time of Isadora Duncan and Mozart. She sees them in portraits, frozen in time. But now they are dead, though Mozart's work is immortal. Just as in earlier poems she wonders about the beauty of a flower that lasts only a few days or a few weeks.

Fair questions, are they not? Why so much beauty, so much design, so much talent, so much hunger, if it is all to be wiped out? Do You or whatever exists that we call You delight in these creatures and then don't miss them when they fade? Like we admire the snow on the mountain side this morning, knowing that it will be gone by noon? Even Mozart — while we celebrate the music, we hardly mourn the troubled, haunted man who created it. Indeed, is there not a certain "romance" in his blend of greatness and a short life? Who cares about his personal sufferings as he died of "military fever," whatever that was?

My wager, my gamble (à la Pascal) is that You care about even the flowers of the field and the birds of the air and that You care far more about us, O we of little faith.

Nonetheless it is all mystery, is it not? Deep, dark mystery. All we can do is trust and hope as our years run out and try to make the most of the great gifts You have given us, trying to be confident that they are promises of even greater gifts. I love You.

January 8, 1997 — Tucson

My Love,

The creatures are revolting. Nothing works. Now my America Online account has been cancelled, for no reason other than the revolt of the machines. The fax doesn't seem to work either. I can't get through to my office because the phones don't work there either.

We are prisoners of our technology. Who needs faxes, phones, or e-mail? Only those of us who have made our lives dependent on them. Life was easier when we didn't have them? Well, maybe. But now that I have all of these things I guess I need them.

I suppose I must be patient while I get them repaired and not let my impatience get the better of me.

Fax is working again. Thank You for small favors.

I love You — and I thank You for the technology which does make life easier.

January 10, 1997 — Tucson

My Love,

In Szy's [Wislawa Szymborska's] poem this morning she speaks with the voice of Lot's wife, trying to explain that she really didn't look back or if she did it were only for a moment. It's only a legend of course, but it makes You look cruel and arbitrary and that I don't like. It's a wonder to me that You didn't suppress the legend.

On the other hand a lot of things which happen in this world look cruel and arbitrary. As You know I don't believe that You cause them. Rather You cannot prevent them and eventually You wipe away every tear. Often it takes a long time for the tears to dry — like those of the D.C. family whose sixteen-year old daughter was killed by a drunken diplomat from Georgia (former Soviet). Why do we need diplomats from that terrible place?

Anyway that looks cruel and arbitrary. The kid is all

right now, I firmly believe. Her family? Will they ever recover?

There's no figuring You out, and I will only get a headache if I try. All I can do is make a leap of faith and figure that in the end You will set all things right.

Otherwise our existence wouldn't make much sense, would it? But what do I know? I love You.

January 13, 1997 — Tucson

My Love,

I'm back from twenty-four-hours in Chicago for the Goggin silver anniversary. Coldest twenty-four hours in recent years, though I was minimally affected by it since I was in cars and houses most of the time.

But the anniversary was a good experience. Wonderful. Gail proposed the toast and was both smooth and funny. Upstaged Terry, which was fine with him. Thank You for giving me the opportunity to participate. I told the strawberry story which all loved.

'Tis still good to be a priest and to be able to participate in such events. I love You.

January 15, 1997 — Tucson

My Love,

Another restless night. I've been working too hard I guess as I try to discharge a lot of sociological obligations which have rested on the back burner. Two new brief pieces, one on social capital and one on the nonpolarization of Catholics, the latter of which will get me in a lot of trouble with the left and the right, both of whom would like there to be polarization for their own purposes. Well, that's what sociology is supposed to be about, *nego majorem* to both sides, and a plague on both your houses.

Szy in her poem today mourns (sort of) the death of a beetle and sees in it the prevalence of death every-where. She is really very good, richly deserves her Nobel Prize, and is profoundly Catholic (i.e., sacramental) even though she may not know it — just like my friend Seamus Heany. Also she is profoundly Polish, just as Seamus is profoundly Irish.

Normally we would walk by the dead insect without noticing it (save perhaps for a brief semi-conscious touch of pathos). She mourns the poor little creature and also mourns for us who must also die, much more spectacu-larly. That is the truth against which my dreams struggle. It is useful to understand. It is also, I think, useful to con-tinue with one's work despite the unconscious mourning. What else are we to do?

Except to throw ourselves completely on Your love and mercy — with as much hope as we can muster.

I love You.

January 16, 1997 — Tucson

My Love,

I've been reading Peter O'Dwyer's book on Irish spiri-tuality, a fascinating treasure trove. He concludes by say-ing that among the traits of Irish spirituality are thin boundaries between this world and the next and between You and Your people. These are certainly fair conclusions. They reveal powerful traits of pre-Christian Irish culture which were especially open to being "baptized." He might have added that the Irish have an incorrigible propensity to express their spiritual insights in poetry, a trait that has surely not disappeared. I know the Irish Church (i.e., bishops and priests) is smart enough to use these resources, though clericalism is still powerful there. On the other hand, new data (at last) from our round-the-world Pope study show that the Irish and the Spanish are the most democratic of all the six peoples we studied. But that's the laity.

One of the advantages of reading about Irish spirituality is that you get to know the Irish writers, because in their poetry they reveal more about themselves than do prose writers. I found myself lamenting that these brave, faithful men and women had to die, as Patrick Pierce, watching happy young children at play, lamented that they too would grow old and die.

It has been a powerful and moving experience for me to read this book because it tells me so much about myself. I hope I learn from it just how close You are to me in the world of nature, in the "black birds" who abound in Irish poetry and spirituality. I'm not sure what they are, and I don't think we have them here, but still You lurk everywhere and I must be more open and more sensitive to Your presence. Help me. I love You.

January 17, 1997 — Tucson

My Love,

First day of class today. It lasted only an hour or so and I was pretty tired at the end. However, it went well. The students seemed interested; some of them I fear are fans and think I'm wonderful. You do too, but then You're prejudiced and so am I. Anyway I must not disillusion them too completely in class. I love You.

January 19, 1997 — Tucson

My Love,

First Mass at Our Mother of Sorrows this Sunday morning. Impressive crowd, full church, nice people, like the way I do Mass — so friendly and open they say.

That's what it's supposed to be of course. I don't know why more of us don't do it that way. Maybe because we are afraid to creep out from behind our clerical masks. Or we do so by fiddling with the words and the gestures, which I suspect annoys more than it pleases.

Anyway, I always feel good about a liturgy like that, as I'm supposed to feel because the liturgy is supposed to console, reassure, challenge, and unite. Even badly done it has a powerful impact, on both people and celebrant — Durkheim's *representation collectif.*

Today is the first nice Arizona day, for which many thanks.

And indeed many thanks for the opportunity to come here each year. I love You.

January 20, 1997 — Tucson

My Love,

In her poem this morning Szy describes a medieval miniature in which a duke and a duchess and knights and ladies, all attractive, all well dressed, ride up to a gorgeous, towering castle. Then in the next frame they're all in hell!

Typical medieval spirituality, doubtless shaped in part by what the various plagues, especially the black death, did to the young and rich and handsome as well as to the old and the poor and the ugly. Certainly it was a time when men and women could easily smell the sulfur of the fires of hell. No Origen speculating about the universality of salvation, as even some of the present Pope's favorite theologians do.

In our day, we give a good deal more credit to Your Mercy and Your Love. Does that make us overconfident? Are we happier that Hell has been reduced to a hypothesis and the devil to a mythological fiction and sexual pleasure to a grace?

I think we probably are. Maybe there is not enough fear of the Lord, which is the beginning of wisdom (albeit only the beginning). Maybe presumption is more widespread than it used to be.

Yet I prefer a God whose justice is subordinate to His (or, better Her) love, a God who can pragmatically get around stubborn human freedom, a God, truth to tell, like the one in my novel *Angel Song*.

Are You that kind of God? Either You are or You're not God and there is some more ultimate creature that is pure love. Modern humankind doesn't want a God who is not pure love, and I think that's right. Would that the Church could preach You that way more often.

January 22, 1997 — Tucson

My Love,

Yesterday was a very rough day. Lots of things came together at once while I as trying to do my daily two thousand words on the new Blackie novel. The big event was a letter from the President about *Irish Lace* which I add herein for the record so I won't forget it, though You knew about it before I did and in the instant he wrote it (I can't figure out how You do those things, but that's besides the point).

THE WHITE HOUSE
WASHINGTON

January 10, 1997

The Reverend Andrew M. Greeley
National Opinion Research Center
1155 East 60th Street
Chicago, Illinois 60637

Dear Father Greeley:
   Irish Lace was wonderful. I greatly enjoyed it, as I
do all your books, and I'd love to have a copy of the
new one, *Irish Whisky*.
   Thanks, too, for the mention in *Irish Lace* — I had
noticed it.

Sincerely,
Bill Clinton

   So that was very nice, the ultimate in jacket blurb, if
you will — short of the Pope! The problem then arose as
to whether we can use it in publicity. Certainly not without the permission of the White House. However every
one was so excited yesterday that they cooked up various schemes without my knowing about it. So there was
all kinds of crisis stuff. My stomach became upset with
nerves, which is a rare enough event in my life. My own
mind is made up; we cannot exploit the President. Enough
other people do that. On the other hand if the White
House gives permission, it would be wonderful.
   Anyway the letter was awfully nice and I'm happy he
likes my books.
   Thank You for that grace.
   I love You. Help me to settle down today.

January 25, 1997 — Tucson

My Love,

A new Durkin, number 11, one Patrick Mallory Durkin, perhaps to be called Paddy. Thank You for the miracle of life.

Speaking of miracles, I was sent a book on miracles to review. As I glanced at it I had to ask myself what I believe about miracles.

First, the greatest miracle of all is that there is anything at all, something utterly beyond the laws of nature.

The second miracle is the miracle of love, why creatures should be able to love.

Having said those things I ask myself, Do You intervene with events that are beyond the laws of nature, to which I reply, What are the laws of nature? Do we know them, will we ever know them? Our cosmos is too mysterious, too complex, too filled with marvel and wonder to exclude anything. Who knows what can happen, what has happened, what will happen? Do miracles happen all the time, are You intervening all the time in the interstices of the cosmos?

I think it unwise to deny You any power at all. Who knows what You can do when You want to? However, in practice I am also skeptical of all claims to specific miracles. Because I refuse to believe that the possibility for marvel has been excluded from the universe, I am not therefore constrained to believe in specific and highly dubious claims for marvels. So I'm agnostic on the subject of miracles. I simply don't know what goes on and am a skeptic about most alleged miracles. I don't think they prove anything. They are signs and wonders. Jesus himself was dubious about the quest for signs and wonders. Yet there were certainly signs in his life and there are signs today (if not all that many). The question perhaps ought to be of what they are signs rather than whether You violate the laws of nature.

So I *do* believe in the miracle of Your love.

Which I try to return everyday of my life.

January 29, 1997 — Tucson

My Love,

I ate supper last night with a good friend from Chicago. He had lots of positive feedback for me, as did a Chicagoan who was eating near us at El Charro.

My friend, who is something of a conservative, says bishops have been afraid of me and with reason, but that I should keep them afraid of me in order to protect the people.

I don't see myself in that role. I certainly receive little support, except for praise on elevators and street corners, and that provides no power. The clergy pretend I don't exist. I am not a Chicago icon as the AJC [American Jewish Committee] people claim I am.

I don't know what to make of this stuff. There is so much negative feedback I tend to discount the positive stuff. Part of my personality, I guess. I have no sense of where I am in these matters. Maybe I don't value my position enough. I just don't know.

I am confused, as You can tell. I certainly will not attack the new Archbishop on his arrival. I don't even know who he will be. But as time goes on, I cannot preclude any possibility. I must be open.

But that's a transient issue. The larger issue of who and what I am in my home city is obscure. I need guidance. Help me, please.

February 1997

❦

February 4, 1997 — Chicago

My Love,

There is thick fog today. I realize how much I hate dark weather only after I return from Tucson, where the sun shines more often. But You are the God of fog as well as light, the God of youth as well as age, the God of winter as well as summer, of hope as well as fear, of celebration as well as loneliness, of night as well as day; whatever is, in some fashion is You, and I love You in all Your manifestations.

February 5, 1997 — Chicago

My Love,

Sixty-nine years old today! That's pretty old isn't it!

I don't feel that old, whatever "that old" is.

I am grateful for every one of those years of my life, for every month, every week, every day, every hour, every minute, every second. You have blessed me abundantly. My life has been exciting beyond my wildest dreams. There have been bad moments, bad times, terrible experiences, but the good has so far outweighed the bad as to

165

be mind-boggling. There are those who hate me, most of them for what they think I am or what they have turned me into; but far more people love me. I am grateful to You for them and for all my family and friends. I am grateful for my parents whose pictures this morning, quite by chance if there is anything such as chance, are on either side of my computer monitor. They brought me into the world and richly endowed me with faith and dedication and love.

I do not know what lies ahead. Surely there won't be nearly as many birthdays as there have been. I will try to treasure each year and live it as best as I can for You. Help me to continue to seize the opportunities and to love even as I am loved.

Take care of me, I beg You.

I love You. I thank You for thrusting me into life as part of this wonderful love affair for which You create. Grant that I may always try to respond to Your love.

February 8, 1997 — Chicago

My Love,

I finished the Blackie novel yesterday in a burst of work, determined to get it done even if it took all day, which it did. It was right on schedule, forty days, eighty thousand words, two thousand a day. It was great fun as You know, tricks and teases and twists and red herrings and false clues — and all the time of course absolute fair play with the reader. Subplots and counterplots and ironies and comedy.

I will be described again, I suppose, as a writing machine. So what! It is a fun story. Most readers will enjoy it and profit from it. So thank You for the fun of writing it and for the talent that makes me a storyteller and the improvement of that talent with each book. Help me to continue to write fiction and to continue to improve. May my stories also continue to be a way of teaching about Your love for us.

I love You.

February 15, 1997 — Tucson

My Love,

I read during the week David Toolan's article in *Cross Currents* about cosmology and spirituality. It emphasized the enormity of Your work and incredible power which can produce such work. It's a brilliant and powerful article. He too notes the paradox of how You are so immensely powerful and yet want to be known as Love and even as a Lover. In fact, or so it seems to me, You want and even need to be Love and a Lover. For all Your immense power You are still a vulnerable God.

There are a lot of unresolved mysteries, and there always will be. Science will not figure everything out. Indeed science and a theological reflection like Toolan's make the world a more wondrous, fascinating place, but even more mysterious. However, as I have often said in these reflections, a God that is not mysterious is not a God worth believing in.

It is almost mad to assume, as I have in all these reflections, that You are accessible as a "thou," as a "lover." But it is Your invitation, is it not? An invitation which revelation confirms but which seems to exist on the "edge" of reality, a hint of great, consuming, passionate love!

I believe that, not strongly enough, as You well know. But I still believe it. Even on this peaceful Saturday morn-

ing in which I'd much rather sit outside in the sun than
work on mail and phone calls.

Anyway I love You.

February 16, 1997 — Tucson

My Love,

Busy day for a Sunday. Pretty much caught up on
everything however. Always catch up. We helped couples
to renew their marriage vows at Mass this morning. So
much love in people's eyes. You lurk in that love, perhaps
more than in almost any other metaphor we have available
in the world. Why doesn't the Church seem to grasp that
and then help them sustain the love?

Especially because we have the symbol system that
should be enormous help to them.

I must try, somehow, someway.

I love You. Help me to love You more.

February 17, 1997 — Tucson

My Love,

I'm catching up on my reading these days and pil-
ing up more books. The house is filled with them. As I
glanced at the stacks this morning I wondered what point
there has been in all the reading. Certainly I've learned
a lot and maybe relaxed a lot, but it all seems kind of
pointless today.

I'll keep on reading of course because I'm an addicted
reader and because I always think that in a given book
I'm going to learn something good or useful. I'm usually
wrong, but it is worth the effort, I guess.

My brain is as filled with useless or quasi-useless information as this house is filled with books.

Again I have that gnawing question of whether I've wasted my life. Most of the causes I have fought for are lost causes. Much of the work I've done has had little impact. Admittedly my novels have had a positive impact on lots of people. Still the feeling of profound failure haunts me whenever I stop to think about it — and this morning I'm not particularly tired either.

What can I tell You?

But it's too late to quit. I'm not sure what would happen if I tried. We all make mistakes. I've made more than my share. Most of them can't be undone.

The phone is disrupting my reflections. Bad morning.

I do love You.

February 18, 1997 — Tucson

My Love,

I went off to the movies last night for the first time since I've been here to see *Breaking the Waves*, a Danish film of the same general sort as *Babette's Feast*. As Roger Ebert in his review (which I dug up at 11:30 last night) nicely puts it, the film argues that not only do You see everything but understand a lot more than we normally give You credit for.

At first I thought that the bearded Calvinist elders in the Church were a bit over the wall in their stern moralizing and their eagerness on their own authority to damn a congregant to hell. Then I realized how many priests and bishops (and Popes) are willing to be just as stern, just as righteous, just as harsh, even though technically not Calvinists. They seem so confident that they have a monopoly on Your Spirit — such that She can no longer blow whither She will.

Idolatry!

I am loyal to the Church, as You well know. But that does not require me to say that there is no hypocrisy, phoniness, prejudice, fraud, and deceit in it. It is made up of humans who are often no better than they have to be, which isn't very good. Then they cloak their ambition and power lust in the aura of the sacred and demand something that approaches worship.

Films like *Breaking the Waves* shatter us because they suggest that You are a good deal more flexible and loving than are many church leaders. I certainly believe that. I think I have learned through the years about the importance of not trying to contain Your Spirit. Sometimes, however, one doesn't get much support for that even from the supposed liberals.

Anyway the film made a deep impression on me and confirms the image I have of You. Yet the image is still inadequate, not by excess but by defect. You are far more loving and forgiving than the God of *Breaking the Waves*. Hence my love for You is so much less than You deserve.

Yet I do love You.

February 20, 1997 — Tucson

My Love,

Mike Hout and I have been working all day on our papal election paper, which I have sent off to the *Tablet* already. I hope they use it. It's important.

This has been a good two months for articles — *Tablet, American Behavioral Science, America, The American Prospect.*

Now if "God in the Movies" makes it to the *New York Times*, it will be a sweep.

I should feel good about these things, but for some reason I don't.

Shame on me.

I love You. Help me to love You more.

February 22, 1997 — Tucson

My Love,

I'm reading John Polkinghorne's *Searching for Truth* again. His meditations are uneven, but when they're good, they're very good. He tells this morning about the mathematician Paul Cardwell who searched for beautiful mathematical formulae because he felt that they were the ones that were most likely to reflect the way the universe works. I have no idea what math beauty is, but I'm sure that it's like all beauty — splendor of the form in the proportioned parts of the matter.

You not only know higher math, as Einstein said, but You also know the formulae which are most likely to strike our minds as beautiful. What an odd coincidence!

Or as Chesterton would have said, perhaps it is a plot. Hence there must be a plotter! And a very ingenious plotter indeed!

What more wonderful plots will we discover?

February 23, 1997 — Tucson

My Love,

Two kicks in the stomach yesterday. After Mass I was shaking hands with people in the back of church, most of whom loved both the story and the cheerful informality with which I try to celebrate the eucharistic meal. A woman came by and said, "Nice show, Father!" I winced because it isn't supposed to be a show, but, naïf that I am, I didn't think she was trying to be nasty. Then when she had walked behind me so that I could not reply, she snapped, "Just remember that Jesus is supposed to be the show, not you!"

Uh-huh. Then when I got back to the sacristy there was a (signed, but no return address) letter from a man who accused me of being a habitual drunk and saying Mass drunk.

As You well know, I don't drink much (a glass of wine, a sip of Bailey's) and have never been drunk.

In both cases, they don't like the way I preside over the Eucharist. Drink and Jesus are only excuses for their fury.

I try to make the Eucharist a family dinner celebration, which I take it to be, a celebration of the risen Jesus. As such I try to draw the kids into it as much as I can. I admit that I enjoy the Eucharist when I preside in that fashion. If we are celebrating resurrection, should we not be joyous? I sometimes wonder if I go too far, though the overwhelming reaction from people suggests that they don't think so.

I have argued on the basis of data that one should not believe that letters from crazies are typical. There is not, I contended, a mass of people out there who think like the crazies do. They do not represent any but a tiny minority. To concede them even a reply is to give them too much. You can't expect that everyone will like you. You have to expect that the crazies will malign you. It goes with the territory. I would be a coward if I let myself be intimidated by the craziness. Yet it does hurt. But being hurt goes with the territory too.

Anyway I'm over it after writing these reflections. Nonetheless, the crazies have a lot of influence in Rome.

Protect me from them, please.

I love You.

February 24, 1997 — Tucson

My Love,

I had an interesting evening last night — and a depressing one — with one of my classmates who left the priesthood. He has had a tough life and has been treated shabbily by the Church, which wasted his talents twice. Why do we have to be so stupid, so mean, so nasty, so envious? I don't think it's still that way with those who have left the active ministry. Rather there is a great deal more tolerance. Yet the priesthood, like everything else, tends to become an end in itself when it should be only a means. I've had my share of problems with it, though I have not left the priesthood. Many would like to see me go, I suppose.

All in all, it was depressing. So many opportunities have been lost since the Council, almost all of them needlessly so. We thought we would get a reform and we did not. So we still need reform, and we won't get it till we change the way we elect Popes and appoint bishops. That will be a long time coming.

I love You. Give me new spirit for the trip to North Carolina.

March 1997

March 1, 1997 — Tucson

My Love,

Back home. Tired from the trip. Nonetheless I praise You for giving us humans the ability to fly all the way across a continent in a rain storm and still be only two hours late. Not so long ago it would have taken a couple of months and even more recently a couple of days. However, in those times I would not have tried to travel from here to Hendersonville, N.C.

The talks went well. They liked what I did. Most of them had read my novels, understood them, and enjoyed them.

I was impressed by the Episcopalians. They are nice people, sing with wonderful enthusiasm, and can impart a dignity to simple liturgy that is very nice. Their bishop was a cut above most of ours. I find myself wondering why our bishops are so inferior. The answer is that they are not elected by their priests and people. We simply have to change this practice if reform in the Church will ever succeed.

I love You. Help me to love You more.

175

March 4, 1997 — Tucson

My Love,

Bishop Bill McManus died last night, the end of an era, the era of brilliant graduates from our seminary, of gifted and able bishops, of confident men of the Church. I know he's already home with You. Take good care of him for us until we all meet again.

The story from Sunday was of a woman whose husband was badly embalmed two years ago. There was odor from the body at Mass and flies around his tomb at the cemetery. They removed his body and won't bury it again. She must agree to cremation. She believed that cremation was against the teaching of the Church (in part as I later learned from Tom because she had been away from the Church for a long time and wasn't up on the new rules). I tried to explain that the rule against cremation was only a rule and could be and was in fact changed and that cremation was all right now. She half believed me, I think. Anyway I put her mind at rest for the moment and was sympathetic and supportive.

The poor woman. Bad enough to lose a husband but with that gruesome stuff added to the burden. Small wonder that she was in bad shape. Take care of her please. There is nothing I can do.

The phone and fax are going crazy. I love You.

March 10, 1997 — Tucson

My Love,

Today I thank You and praise You for the taste of cranberry juice, a glass of which the good Monsignor gave me after Mass and before my lecture yesterday afternoon. How wonderful it was!

I'm liking juices these days I guess!

"Star of the South, give us great love," my book of Celtic Wisdom says today. Oh, yes, great love. I need the predisposition and time to love You with a great love. Star of the South, give me great love!

March 12, 1997 — Tucson

My Love,

Today I praise You for the mountains, especially the Catalinas behind my house and the glorious rose they turn at sunset. I also thank You for this the first day of my own spring break.

I also praise You today for music and especially for the wondrous music of *Traviata*, which I heard last night. What a wonderful and gratuitous gift music is. We didn't have to have it, but we do in fact have it, another hint of Your wonder and goodness. I thank You for it.

Help me to love You more.

March 16, 1997 — Tucson

My Love,

Today I celebrate the power of the liturgy to lift up one's spirits and give new meaning and purpose in life, even when one is on sinus medicine.

I will miss Tucson when I go home. This has been the best time here ever in terms of faculty and university. Thank You for that too.

You know why I must hurry.

I love You.

March 19, 1997 — Tucson

My Love,

The Bernardin book, *Gift of Peace,* which I read yesterday, was deeply moving. It also made me feel sad because
I erred so often in my relationship with him. Yet in fact,
given my naivete and my relative powerlessness, there
was not all that much I could have done anyway. There
were people who were afraid of me and who wanted to
keep us isolated one from another and there really wasn't
much I could do to stop them. I was an outsider in the
Archdiocese and I always will be, and there's nothing I
can do about that.

I thank You that Joe and I were friends again during
the final years.

I love You.

March 23, 1997 — Tucson

My Love,

I thank You and praise You this morning for the desert
and all its wild and weird plants, which prove once again
that You are a jokester.

I was fine at the Eucharist yesterday, which proves that
it was indeed the medicine and not general deterioration
which did me in the previous week. I suppose that will
happen eventually, but at least not now.

I accept whatever You have in store for me.

I am still struggling with the Bernardin years, trying
to make sense of them all.

I love You.

March 24, 1997 — Tucson

My Love,

Today I praise You and thank You for friends, especially those who were at the party last night.

I also reflect finally on the Bernardin years in Chicago and conclude that there is no reason for fighting Your Spirit. The schemers who kept us apart wasted their time and energy, and while I still can't understand their fears and hatred, I was a lot better off precisely in the role I played.

How many times before have I come to that conclusion?

I wonder if perhaps my most important work lies ahead of me.

I love You.

March 26, 1997 — Tucson

My Love,

I thank You and praise You for the wind which is blowing fiercely outside. Like many other phenomena it can be destructive, but without it we'd all die of air stagnation. Just now it feels very good.

I'm packing to go home. Not much fun, but then it never is.

I continue to ponder what, if anything, You have planned for me for the rest of my life. Have I done my part, played my role, fulfilled my responsibilities as a writer and a storyteller and a priest? Or is there something that remains to be done?

If it is merely the former, if my future is merely to analyze data, write stories, and preside over the Eucharist,

I surely have no complaints. It has been an exciting life and I am grateful. If on the other hand there is more to be done, help me to recognize Your Spirit when She appears. Help me also to keep my anger under control and avoid all unnecessary conflicts.

I love You.

March 27, 1997 — Tucson

My Love,

I thank You today and praise You for calling me to the priesthood, a feast of which today is, at least in some part.

And I reflect how little there is left today of the priestly mystique and ideology with which I was raised. We are not a band of brothers, but rather a band of envious arrogant incompetents (not all priests, surely, but certainly the clerical culture of the priesthood). We are not loyal to one another. We are not skilled professionals. We are bemused by our own claims to sacred power. We do not serve our people well — witness the poor quality of our sermons. We don't hold God in our hands. We have to earn respect and often we fail to do that. We are mediocrities. Some of us sexually abuse those over whom we have power. We are often rude, crude, insensitive. Yet, paradoxically, enough of the laity need us more than ever, even if we don't understand the need for them. There are also many wonderful priests, even if often they are nearly submerged in the mediocrity of clerical culture. The mystique is gone, but the demands and the importance of the role remain. If only more of us could see it that way.

So today, as I prepare for Holy Thursday at one of the best parishes in America, I renew my priestly commitment and pray for all priests. Help me to become a better priest than I am.

I love You.

March 28, 1997 — Good Friday, Tucson

My Love,

The saddest day of the year, they used to call this. It is appropriate to mourn the suffering Your Son endured, even if he triumphed over it. We mourn every death (and there are so many!), so all the more we should mourn the death of the innocent one. I thank You and praise You for sending him to show us how to live and how to die and thus to create the context and make possible our own ultimate triumph over sin and death.

As You know I have trouble with such concepts as redemption and salvation and sacrifice. To say nothing of propitiation. I accept them in whatever sense they are taught, but I really don't know how to explain them. I think that St. Anselm somehow stands in the way of understanding in our day. I do however understand the image and the story behind those words — the story of self-sacrificing love for us. Beyond that everything else is explication.

Jesus had to die because he was human, but he didn't have to die the way he did. The manner of his death, however, certainly does clarify for us how horrible death is and how generous You are. He showed us how to live and how to die. Through him You went down to the valley of death with us. What an astonishing thought! Not new, surely, but never fully comprehended. Help me to understand it better and live more richly in it, because I too must die. Horribly, because all death is horrible.

This final packing to go back to Chicago is a minor death experience and the return to Chicago will be, when I'm there, a minor resurrection experience. Help me to learn the meaning of that truth.

March 30, 1997 — Chicago

My Love,

Back home and it's good to be home, especially with the sun appearing and turning the whole city an Easter gold in this late afternoon. I praise and thank You for having a city to come home to, and such a beautiful one at that. I am, as usual, disoriented. Like I went out today without my wallet. However it is a small price to pay for the rewards of having two cities. I can move from one kind of life to another on this beautiful spring day.

At the party today all of the grand nieces and nephews: young life, new life (newest of all, Kellianne, just barely walking, and Paddy, brand new). They are life who will be around long after I'm gone, and I celebrate the continuity of life and the promise of more life which they represent.

March 31, 1997 — Chicago

My Love,

I thank You and praise You today for the lovely city spread out beneath in the glow of spring sunlight.

I love You, even when I feel spiritually drained as I do today. I need a day of recollection. I hereby set Sunday as one such day.

Help me to stick to that resolution.

April 1, 1997 — Chicago

My Love,

I sing Your praises for superabundant beauty. Beauty is restored from the south, from the north, from the east, from the west, as the Navajo prayer I read this morning suggests.

So much beauty everywhere, buildings, flowers, trees, sky, the touch of a spring breeze, human beauty, Help me to see in it these spring days a hint of You, the source of all beauty.

Help me to be sensitive to beauty wherever it appears, as, for example, in the first tiny sprout of green in the flower arrangements around our building or in the Easter lily in my apartment, even in the smell of the lily.

I love You.

April 3, 1997 — Chicago

My Love,

Well, I have 140 students in my class, because the registrar lifted the limit, without consulting me. It's going to be difficult. All I could do would be to cancel the class, but I can't do that to the students. Priest that I am, I'm a sucker for young people.

Yesterday we saw *All that Jazz* in class. A different view of death.

Is death a friend, like Joe said, quoting Henri Nouwen?

Is death You, as Bob Fosse thought it might be? If it is, then it surely is a friend.

Anyway I praise You and thank You for the enthusiasm and the hope of students, even if there are so many of them around just now. I love You.

April 6, 1997 — Chicago

My Love,

Daylight saving time! How wonderful! The sunshine is no longer wasted on early morning but will go into the evening! I praise You and thank You for daylight and for daylight saving and for spring and summer and for the brightness in my life.

I also thank You for the graces of yesterday's day of recollection. The most important impact of a day like yesterday is that it slows me down, forces me to realize that I don't have to work at the pace I've been working, that indeed most days do not have to be hectic. I'm going to try to adjust my life, both spiritual and physical, to a somewhat different pace. — one day off a week, no working in the evening. Minor stuff, I realize, but the difference it makes in my prayer life is always enormous.

I can't do that every day, as this week will demonstrate, but I can do it on a number of days.

And if I do, then I too can live and act more like a herald of joy, which is the role I should have in life.

I love You.

April 9, 1997 — Chicago

My Love,

Well, as You know, the new bishop is Francis "Pat" George, appointed after less than a year in Portland and six years in Yakima. Maybe he will grow in the job; I hope he's not too smart to learn. One must give him a chance.

As for me forty-three years a priest now and not that far away from retirement. Why worry about the new Archbishop? Why worry about anything?

But that's not who I am. I will keep on trying as long as You give me health and life. Today I am merely conscious that life is not very long and could be very short. I continue my work while I can.

I love You.

April 14, 1997 — Chicago

My Love,

Warming up finally, beautiful day, beautiful city — for all of which I thank You and praise You.

Yesterday I read The *Healing Power of Stories* by Daniel Taylor, a wonderful book which says that we are our stories. I asked myself what are my principal stories. Here are some of them:

1. St. Angela, the Great Depression, the War, and the postwar world.

2. Second grade, Quigley, Mundelein, Christ the King, the University.

3. Cardinal Meyer, then Cody, and then an outcast. Joe left me there as the new man probably will too.

4. Polyani, Geertz, James, Shea, Tracy, storytelling.

5. My discovery that You could be imagined across gender.

6. Jim Miller, Bernie Geis, novels.

Gosh, with stories like that who has any reason to complain about life. I've written all of this in my memoir, but it's good to recall it.

Thank You for exciting, exciting stories!

April 15, 1997 — Chicago

My Love,

There apparently is a rumor floating around on the Internet that I died last week. As far as I know, that isn't true! Do You know anything about it?

I love You.

April 25, 1997 — Chicago

My Love,

In the book in honor of Michael Buckley, *Finding God in All Things*, I learned more about the debate concerning how You are present in the world. However it is resolved, I do believe that You are present everywhere, present and listening! Please listen to me today, my love, and help me to listen to You.

April 26, 1997 — Chicago

My Love,

I have been reflecting on how every Archbishop since Meyer has heard me attacked before coming to Chicago.

Meyer alone dismissed the attackers. I'm sure the new man will also hear plenty of attacks before he comes. I gather that a young priest in a suburban parish denounced me from the altar for what I was alleged to have said (he didn't hear me) on TV the day of the appointment. So that will be the new distortion. So be it.

I had pretty much decided not to do the commentary on Archbishop George's installation. Now I think I will, just to defy those like the idiot priest who denounced me for simply raising a question about the new bishop's administrative experience.

Not very peaceful thoughts this morning, are they? Sorry about my mood.

I love You.

April 29, 1997 — At La Guardia

My Love,

Bob Merton was at the Russell Sage lunch today. He expressed dismay that I had not been elected president of the ASA for my work and the lack of recognition in the profession of my work and of the sociology in my novels.

Well, praise like that from the grand old man of American sociology is a nice thing to have. I won't say it doesn't make any difference because it does encourage me. Being an outcast in both the academy and the Church is not a pleasant matter, not even now. But I have learned the wisdom of not fighting the trajectories of Your Spirit. I am better off where I am and doing what I'm doing. I thank You for the trajectories You have imposed on my life.

I love You.

May 1997

May 2, 1997 — Chicago

My Love,

A new book of Celtic (Highland) prayers. Truly great. It begins with a creed which is a morning prayer to the "Great God of all Gods." I don't think the title suggests that there are any others, but then You know that. Toward the conclusion are these wonderful lines:

> *My thought, my deed, my word, and my will,*
> *My mind, my brain, my state, and my way,*
> *I beseech thee to keep me from ill*
> *To keep from hurt and from harm today*
> *To keep me from grieving and from plight*
> *In thy love's nearness to keep this night.*

A prayer for getting up and going to bed! How lovely. And how trusting the belief, what confidence in You and Your power. I believe in that power and in Your love.

Even when I am as tired as I am this morning. I love You. Help me.

May 4, 1997 — Chicago

My Love,

I thank You and praise You for the good night of sleep last night and for the good day today. I'm up tomorrow at four o'clock to be off at five for the trip to D.C. Great way to celebrate my forty-third anniversary in the priesthood! I certainly would not have thought on that day so long ago that I'd be spending this day in the Russell Senate Office Building defending the General Social Survey.

Surprise, surprise, surprise!

Thank You for all the surprises. Grant that I may always be open to them.

And may I make my own as I set out on the ten days of travel the Celtic prayer I read today:

> *May God shield me, and may God fill*
> *Oh, may God watch me and may God hold*
> *Oh, may God bring me where peace is still*
> *to the king's land, eternity's fold.*

I make those my prayers today and tomorrow and all the days of my life as I continue, celebrating I hope, in the priesthood.

May 5, 1997 — On the plane to D.C.

My Love,

Forty-three years a priest today! For that grace I give You much thanks and high praise. The grace isn't what it used to be. Much of the myth of the band of brothers is gone, as is the automatic respect. Both of these are no real loss. Moreover our image has been hurt terribly by the sex abusers. Some of the reasons many of us had in becoming priests, are no longer valid. Yet the core of the role of mediator has not changed and indeed is more important than ever. Moreover most of us find the priesthood even better than we had expected it to be, despite the whiners and the complainers.

As I said to You last night I did not expect forty-three years ago to be on a plane to D.C. this morning, but that is part of the priestly role I try to play. I am grateful for the blessings and opportunities of the past years and for the gifts You have so lavishly bestowed on me. I'm sorry for the mistakes, the errors, the discouragement, and the anger which have made me less effective as a mediator than I might have been. I rededicate myself to my ministry as a priest for however many years remain in Your generosity. Help me to avoid past mistakes and be a more effective witness to Your love.

I love You. Thanks once again for the priesthood.

ALSO BY

ANDREW M. GREELEY

WINDOWS

"You will need to hike a country mile before you find a book more
delightful to read and more helpful in your personal spirituality.
A terrific book, just wonderful!" — *The Catechist's Connection*

0-8245-1517-X; $14.95

SACRAMENTS OF LOVE

"Many Christians, not by any means only Roman Catholics, will be
inspired, perhaps even transformed, by the courage, optimism, and
depth of these meditations that point beyond Greeley to God,
hidden and revealed." — *Library Journal*

0-8245-1594-3; $14.95

LOVE AFFAIR

"An eye-opener. The journal's impact is revelatory not only of the
nature of prayer but of Andrew Greeley himself." — *ALA Booklist*

0-8245-1369-X; $10.95

Please support your local bookstore, or call 1-800-395-0690.
For a free catalog, please write us at
THE CROSSROAD PUBLISHING COMPANY
370 LEXINGTON AVENUE, NEW YORK, NY 10017

We hope you enjoyed I Hope You're Listening, God.
Thank you for reading it.

crossroad